'SERIOUS SPORT'

SPORT IN THE GLOBAL SOCIETY
General Editor: J.A. Mangan

The interest in sports studies around the world is growing and will continue to do so. This unique series combines aspects of the expanding study of *sport in the global society*, providing comprehensiveness and comparison under one editorial umbrella. It is particularly timely, with studies in the cultural, economic, ethnographic, geographical, political, social, anthropological, sociological and aesthetic elements of sport proliferating in institutions of higher education.

Eric Hobsbawm once called sport one of the most significant practices of the late nineteenth century. Its significance was even more marked in the late twentieth century and will continue to grow in importance into the new millennium as the world develops into a 'global village' sharing the English language, technology and sport.

Other Titles in the Series

'SERIOUS SPORT'

J.A. Mangan's Contribution to the History of Sport

Editor

Scott A.G.M. Crawford
Eastern Illinois University

FRANK CASS
LONDON • PORTLAND, OR

First published in 2004 in Great Britain by
FRANK CASS PUBLISHERS
Crown House, 47 Chase Side, Southgate,
London, N14 5BP

and in the United States of America by
FRANK CASS PUBLISHERS
c/o ISBS, Suite 300
920 NE 58th Avenue
Portland, Oregon 97213-3644

Website: www.frankcass.com

British Library Cataloguing in Publication Data

'Serious sport': J.A. Mangan's contribution to the history of sport.
– (Sport in the global society)
1.Mangan, J. A. – Contributions in the history of sport
2.Sports – Historiography
I.Crawford, Scott A. G. M. II.Mangan, J. A. III.The international
journal of the history of sport
796'.09

ISBN 0-7146-5569-4 (cloth)
ISBN 0-7146-8451-1 (paper)

Library of Congress Cataloging-in-Publication Data

Serious sport: J.A. Mangan's contribution to the history of sport /
editor, Scott A.G.M. Crawford.
p. cm.
Includes bibliographical references and index.
ISBN 0-7146-5569-4 (cloth) – ISBN 0-7146-8451-1 (paper)
1. Mangan, J. A. 2 Sports – History. I. Mangan, J. A. II. Crawford,
Scott A. G. M. III. Title.
GV571.S47 2004
796'.09–dc22

2003023035

This group of studies first appeared as a special issue of The International
Journal of the History of Sport (ISSN 0952-3367), Vol.20, No.4,
December 2003, published by Frank Cass

Printed in Great Britain by MPG Books Ltd, Bodmin, Cornwall

'Serious sport has nothing to do with fair play. It is bound up with hatred, jealousy, boastfulness, and disregard of all the rules'

George Orwell
Shooting an Elephant (1950)

Contents

Foreword

I am delighted to provide a foreword to this much merited celebratory volume in recognition of the enormous and invaluable contribution J.A. (Tony) Mangan has made to the study of the history of sport.

As Jon Manley relates in his 'Editing with J.A. Mangan' (pp.1–3), Tony brought us the idea of *The British Journal of Sports History* in 1984, over a decade after we published Eric Dunning's pathbreaking *Readings in the Sociology of Sport*.

The contributors to this collection discuss Tony Mangan's innovative and visionary pursuit of the study of imperialism and sport, and his work on militarism and sport, and on sport and the Victorian social classes, but it is the fulsome tributes from his former students, now themselves established and successful academics, which offer real insight into Tony Mangan the man, the teacher, the guide, philosopher and friend, whose faith in them launched their careers as academics and authors.

I always looked forward to editorial meetings with Tony. They were never dull. He always presented his ideas and his views forcefully, rarely taking 'no' for an answer and always adding 'Trust me, Frank, I know what I'm doing' and 'Frank, do it and you will see that it will work'. I invariably did, and it invariably did.

It is an interesting coincidence that I am retiring at the same time as Tony, after completing my first 50 years in the book industry, although I suspect that in both our cases it will mean a diminution of about two per cent of our normal activities.

When we met recently it reminded me of two old-time boxers touching gloves as a sign of mutual respect and affection after finishing a bout, which in our case lasted some 20 memorable and hectic years.

They say that behind every successful man stands an able woman, and I am sure that Doris Mangan, who cooperated with Tony in much of his work, is no exception.

So it gives me great pleasure to join with Tony's family, colleagues and friends in wishing both the 'prizefighter and the bishop' a long, happy and still fruitful future in the years ahead.

FRANK CASS
January 2004

Series Editor's Foreword

Appreciation

More are men's ends marked than their lives before:
The setting sun, and music at the close,
As the last taste of sweets, is sweetest last
Writ in remembrance more than things long past.

William Shakespeare, Richard II, Act 2, Sc. 1, l.11

Reflection

Better the rudest work that tells a story... than the richest without meaning.

John Ruskin, *Seven Lamps of Architecture*,
'The Lamp of Memory', sect. 7

Desire

O! let my books be then the eloquence
And dumb presagers of my speaking breast.

William Shakespeare, Sonnet 23

Ambition

Expect nothing. Live frugally on surprise.

Alice Walker, 'Expect nothing'

From *The Oxford Dictionary of Quotations* [Revised Fourth Edition]
(Oxford: Oxford University Press, 1996) edited by Angela Partington,
pp.619, 550, 633 and 717 respectively

J.A. MANGAN
October 2003

Editing with J.A. Mangan

JONATHAN MANLEY

> *Homo Ludens*, man at play, is surely as significant a figure as man at war or at work. In human activity the invention of the ball may be said to rank with the invention of the wheel. Imagine America without baseball, Europe without soccer, England without cricket, the Italians without bocci, China without Ping-Pong, and tennis for no one.[1]

Nowadays it is almost commonplace to speak of the explosive growth of academic interest in sport and leisure, and several publishers have built impressive lists to meet the demand. The following observations are made from the modest vantage point of a publisher's editor who has had the good fortune to watch this roller-coaster gather momentum and to hitch a short, exhilarating ride.

Frank Cass published Eric Dunning's ground-breaking *Readings in the Sociology of Sport* in 1971, but it was not until 1984 that the company entered the field in earnest by launching *The British Journal of Sports History*. The first issue set out a clear agenda: 'to stimulate, promote and co-ordinate interest in the history of sport, recreation and leisure ... and to advance scholarship in the study of these various aspects of social history by providing a forum for the discussion of new approaches, ideas and information'.[2] Evolving into *The International Journal of the History of Sport* in 1987, it has since become a leading journal in the field and has recently spawned three related journals (*Culture, Sport, Society*; *Soccer and Society*; and *The European Sports History Review*) and a flourishing book series. The energies and abilities of Tony Mangan, executive editor of all these publications, have driven this success.

Professor Mangan has proved the truth of that stale publishing cliché 'You meet the most interesting people'. The cultural historian Jeffrey Richards has characterized him as 'a combination of bishop and prizefighter', an image which captures the proselytizing zeal and bullish determination driving his quest for pioneering scholarship lucidly presented.[3] A passion for clear exposition and jargon-free English has been as vital to the success of *The International Journal of the History of Sport* (and the book series it generated) as scholarly vision and discrimination. A scourge of turgid, unclear, confused and pretentious prose, Mangan is always ready to regale anyone who will listen with the latest barbarism perpetrated by a native English-speaking writer who should know better. He once sent me a *Sunday Telegraph* cartoon of a professor addressing a junior colleague: 'Of course it is possible to express one's ideas in a straightforward coherent manner, but where's the fun in that?' Plain English is not simply desirable, but a requirement – for the benefit of young students who cannot easily, and should not, be forced to attempt to 'digest the indigestible, blatantly pompous or simply poor writing of too many insensitive or inadequate academics'. One such student, defeated by a passage she had read in a textbook, tearfully sought Mangan's help: 'It makes no sense to me either,' he commiserated. 'It's rubbish. The man can't write.' 'He/she can write!' is a compliment he bestows rarely, but always with invigorating enthusiasm.

Mangan's sensitivity to the needs of his students is reflected in his work as an editor. His skill in discovering and nurturing scholars whose first language is not English is famous, but less well known are his tireless efforts (often assisted by his wife Doris, a first-rate copy-editor, proof-reader, indexer and linguist) to make their work presentable. In the interests of advancing scholarship and broadening the international scope of the journals, articles written in opaque English and gibberish would be reworked and patiently honed (sometimes through several drafts) into fluent, often arresting prose (one piece underwent no fewer than 47 versions before being deemed publishable). This work can be satisfying and has been quaintly likened to 'removing layers of crumpled brown paper from an awkwardly shaped parcel, and revealing the attractive present which it contains', but it is frequently tedious, the jewel within eluding even X-ray vision.[4] How many less discriminating and painstaking editors would simply return these multi-layered monstrosities of pidgin English to sender or, worse, consign them to the wastepaper basket?

The success of *The International Journal of the History of Sport* generated a book series, 'Sport in the Global Society', which is truly global in reach, encompassing studies of sport and society in East and South-East Asia, Latin America, Scandinavia, Europe and Africa. In less than six years the series has grown into a list of over 50 titles, two of which have won the prestigious annual prize for best book awarded by the North American Society for Sport History (NASSH).[5] The critical acclaim and commercial success the series has won attest to its general editor's abilities as a writer, editor, trend-spotter and recruiter of academic talent, qualities which have sired a new publishing venture, 'Student Sports Studies'. This book series will introduce the history, sociology and science of sport to younger students. The roller-coaster continues.

NOTES

1. B. Tuchman, *Practising History: Selected Essays* (New York, 1981), p.234, quoted in G. Redmond, 'Sport History in Academe: Reflections on a Half-Century of Peculiar Progress', *British Journal of Sports History*, 1, 1 (May 1984), 38.
2. J.A. Mangan, J. Lowerson and R. Cox, 'Statement from the Editors', *British Journal of Sports History*, 1, 1 (May 1984), iii.
3. Jeffrey Richards speaking at a reception to mark the 15th anniversary of the Frank Cass sports publishing programme, House of Commons, London, 27 Nov. 2001.
4. D. Athill, *Stet: An Editor's Life* (London: Granta Books, 2001), p.37.
5. D. Booth, *The Race Game: Sport and Politics in South Africa* (London and Portland, OR: Frank Cass, 1997) and M. Huggins, *Flat Racing and British Society, 1790–1914: A Social and Economic History* (London and Portland, OR: Frank Cass, 2001).

J.A. Mangan and *The International Journal of the History of Sport*

SCOTT A.G.M. CRAWFORD

More than 25 years ago this writer, living in Dunedin, Otago, was endeavouring to understand the athletic rhetoric that appeared in a number of New Zealand Victorian/Edwardian school magazines. In order to make sense of this material, I searched far and wide for essays in academic journals that explored this terrain. One of these was an October 1975 *British Journal of Educational Studies* (XXIII, 3, October 1975) and a J.A. Mangan said of these types of school magazines that they 'reveal a strangely touching dogmatism and fervour' among a 'unique mixture of emotionalism and innocence, myopia and inflexibility.' Then and now Tony Mangan has been able to use the English language to great effect. His prose has been sustained by a joyous celebration of the art and craft of good writing while avoiding, sometimes by the narrowest of margins, the traps of pedantry and excess erudition.

In the early 1980s Mangan visited the Antipodes and shared with various audiences lecture material drawn from his 1981 Cambridge University Press publication, *Athleticism in the Victorian and Edwardian Public School*. At Otago University, in the South Island of New Zealand, his address was made not to the faculty and students of the School of Physical Education but rather to an eclectic group of history academics. One was an expert on Sikh culture and politics, a second had published on Germany in the 1930s, a third was, arguably, the major authority on the origins of Rhodesia, a fourth had written books on the culture of whaling and navigation history and a fifth was, and continues to be, New Zealand's most significant voice on social class and community. I was present and relished watching a sport historian eyeball, and take on, a group of respected scholars who, *until that moment*, had never seen sport history as either being appropriate or acceptable for historical treatment.

No case is made that Mangan's scholarship won over this group. What is important is that Mangan penetrated a foreign landscape – in this case the field of history not physical education – and brought forward the concept of sport history as worthwhile grist for the academic mill.

A 1982 book review of *Athleticism* described it as a 'tour de force of rigorous historical scholarship' enriched by prodigious notes and a mammoth list of bibliographical sources. Mangan critiqued the poetry of the games cult: H.B. Tristam's writing was 'hearty, well-intentioned propaganda', Edward Bowen's prose was 'jocular silliness' while John Bain's work was illuminated by 'elegiac tenderness'.[1]

In 1990 at the Commonwealth and International Conference on Physical Education, Sport, Health, Dance, Recreation and Leisure (Auckland, New Zealand: 18–23 January) I met up with Mangan for the second time and during several conversations I expressed a strong interest in working with the *IJHS* in some book-reviewing capacity. That connection has continued to the present day and I consistently share with colleagues and students the great pleasure that I have derived from that role.

I am enthused not by the competitive aspects of journal publishing, writing, reviewing, editing, but rather by collegial opportunities to foster sport history and connect to, and communicate with, groups of like minded people all over the world. Contemporary sport history must feel of good heart sustained as it is by not only *The International Journal of the History of Sport* but, among others, the *Journal of Sport History*, the *Sports Historian* (now *Sport in History*), *Sporting Traditions*, *Sport History Review*, and the *British Society of Sports History Newsletter*. In the area of book reviewing I have been much cheered by what the *IJHS* has been able to accomplish. It would be remiss of me, however, if I did not acknowledge the help over the years of Ron Smith of the North American Society for Sport History and his masterly annual NASSH Conference Book List; book review editors Richard Cox (*The Sports Historian*) and Gerry Gems (*The Journal of Sport History*); and Steve Ickringill (*British Society of Sports History*). These three and many others have given wonderfully of their time and support. There have been occasions when one book has been 'double reviewed'. This embarrassment has been happily resolved by other editors willingly taking 'onboard' the review, and seeing it safely harboured and published.

When I was a student at Loughborough College, England, in the 1960s my first exposure to sports history was reading Peter McIntosh.

McIntosh today – deservedly so – is recognized, according to Mike
Huggins, as 'one of a select band of historians of sport who helped
fundamentally to shape the way succeeding historians looked at the
past'[2]. In subsequent years the torch for sport history has shone
brightly for a select group of innovative scholars, among whom
Roberta Park and Allen Guttmann (USA) and Richard Holt, Tony
Mangan and Tony Mason (UK) are pre-eminent. It is not without
significance that the British Society of Sports History through the
vehicle of the *Sports Historian* honoured the life contributions to sport
history made by Tony Mason.[3] Writing a review of Mangan's
Athleticism in 1982 I observed: 'Dr. Mangan's book is a work of
substantial and fluent scholarship. In tandem with Tony Mason's
Association Football and English Society 1863–1915, the study of
Victorian athleticism has scaled new heights.'[4]

The bushy eyebrows, that black thatch of hair and a combative
manner that can be bullying, badgering and used to getting its own way,
makes for a personality that can be either mesmerizing or menacing
depending on your viewpoint. This is a man of no little ego. And as for
his handwriting, despite all manner of bold flourishes, it is consistently
an unintelligible scrawl. All of that notwithstanding, Mangan's
contribution to sport history has been monumental. When I was asked
to be editor of this celebration I positively beamed. I respect Mangan
and, more importantly, the journal that he has nursed and nurtured over
many years – *The International Journal of the History of Sport* – has been
a flagship for all that is worthwhile in our discipline. I will never forget,
for example, the responses of the American sport historian Allen
Guttmann to requests to review many books over the years. If anyone is
prolific and thoughtful, yet hugely busy, it is Guttmann. Without fail he
has agreed to review for the *IJHS*. His reviews are delivered in time,
they are never less than masterly, and he signs off all correspondence
with the phrase, 'Yours affably'. Such a generosity of spirit gladdens
one's heart and convinces me that sport historians are a rare breed of
engaging characters.

Finally, in the twenty-first century what is emerging is a discipline
(sport history) increasingly being energized by clusters of academicians.
In Great Britain alone there is De Montfort University's 'International
Centre for Sports History and Culture' (founded by Wray Vamplew and
now headed by Jeff Hill) and Stirling University's 'Sports Studies and
Research' unit lead by its architect, and founding professor, Grant

Jarvie. It should be noted that predating these two bodies was Tony Mangan's 'International Centre for Sport, Socialisation and Society' based at the then Jordanhill College, now a part of Strathclyde University. As pointed out in this Celebration, Tony Mangan's writing, and indeed the focus of *The International Journal of the History of Sport*, now goes far beyond the bounds of G.E.L. Cotton of Marlborough, Charles Vaughan of Harrow and Edward Thring of Uppingham. As far as I am concerned a good journal bears the personal imprimatur of its editor. It should reflect a commitment to both the publication and the academic field that it showcases. Mangan masterminded the founding of *The International Journal of the History of Sport* and his ongoing enthusiasm in editing that journal and writing about a global canvas should earn him the soubriquet of 'Magellan' Mangan.

I trust that Tony Mangan may enjoy that title and retirement, still several years in the future, as he looks out from his beloved Dorset coast on English seas now home to recreational rather than commercial sailors – the Mangans are now the proud owners of a bungalow in Swanage, 'a sleepy (Rupert Bear) seaside town of the 1930s'. There is every reason to believe that Tony Mangan will, hopefully, keep on writing sport history and that Swanage, England, will be as fruitful for him as Strathclyde, Scotland.

This celebration could well be subtitled 'witty, spirited and robust'. The phrase is taken from Sheldon Rothblatt's glowing tribute to Mangan's second edition of *Athleticism*. It nicely sums up the man and his legacy.

NOTES

1. S.A.G.M. Crawford, a book review of *Athleticism*. *New Zealand Journal of Health, Physical Education and Recreation*, 15, 2 (August 1982), 50–1.
2. M. Huggins, 'Walking in the Footsteps of a Pioneer: Peter McIntosh – Trail-Blazer in the History of Sport,' *The International Journal of the History of Sport*, 18, 2 (June 2001), 136.
3. J. Hill and R. Holt (eds.) 'Sporting Lives: Essays in History and Biography Presented to Tony Mason', *The Sports Historian*, 22, 1 (May 2002).
4. Crawford, *op. cit.*, 51.

3

An Ever-Widening Sphere: J.A. Mangan's Contributions to an Increasingly 'Global' History of Sport

ROBERTA J. PARK

Mike Huggins' tribute to Peter McIntosh, 'Walking in the Footsteps of a Pioneer', which appeared recently in *The International Journal of History of Sport*, is an eloquent and much-needed reminder that in any field of inquiry there are individuals whose scholarship, vision, dedication to task, tenacity, and other qualities have been indispensable in 'leading the way'. Whereas in the 1970s, 'sports history' (sometimes designated as the history of sport or the social history of sport) was only beginning to gain recognition as an academic specialty in various countries, by 2003 it has attained considerable respectability. Courses now are included among the öfferings of departments of history and cultural studies as well as in physical education, long their traditional home. Several university-based research centres organized around the socio/cultural/historical study of sport have been established; leading scholarly journals now regularly review works in the area; comprehensive annual bibliographies are published; several recent encyclopaedias include informative material about the history as well as other dimensions of sport, physical education and related topics among their entries; scholars may consult and/or interact with each other through a number of sport history networks; and major publishing houses now include 'sport history' among their series.

The sea change that has occurred in the last two decades was aptly reflected in former *New York Times* sportswriter Leonard Koppett's introduction to *The Business of Professional Sports* (1991), edited by Paul Staudohar (professor of business administration at California State University, Hayward) and James A. Mangan: 'I think the academics who have been working on sports material, especially the historians, have been providing ... enormously enlightening insights'. By probing beneath and beyond preconceived impressions, these 'pioneers', Koppett continued, were bringing forth much needed insights regarding what was – and is – the 'reality' of sport.[1]

A few years earlier James A. (Tony) Mangan had asked why such an important aspect of modern society (sport) had been 'so inexcusably neglected' and responded to his own question with absolute accuracy:

> The reason is not hard to find ... history like sociology is still essentially Cartesian in implicitly accepting a rigid mind/body dichotomy when philosophy has dismissed the distinction as invalid. ... [I]t is time that sport, like the body, was incorporated within conventional historical debate about ideologies, control, organization, stratification and mobility.[2]

He and others, in fact, already had begun correcting many misconceptions and bringing new understandings to a field of study that had been marginalized, indeed neglected, for far too long by scholars.

Paths that McIntosh 'pioneered' a half-century ago now have been followed by many others: and exciting new ones have been opened up. While credit for this growth belongs to many individuals, there is no one who has made as extensive and far-reaching contributions as Tony Mangan, who has produced a remarkable collection of single-authored and edited works that, taken together, have become truly 'global' in scope. His combined efforts and achievements have been instrumental in bringing to the attention of the general public as well as to the academy the historical study of sport and its multifaceted, often contradictory, and intensely compelling meanings. In an arena that has seen a steady increase in the number of exceptional contributions, his has been an undertaking of *mammoth* proportions. As but one example, the *Catalogue of the National Library of Congress* lists no fewer than 30 volumes that he has authored and edited.

Early in his publishing career, which began with articles like 'Some Sociological Concomitants of Secondary School Physical Education' (in *Research Papers in Physical Education*, 1971) and *Physical Education and Sport: Sociological and Cultural Perspectives* (1973), which he edited and for which he wrote the chapter 'Physical Education as a Ritual Process', there were indications of what soon would become his highly regarded contribution to the study of that dominating sporting ideology – 'athleticism' – and to an ever-widening agenda that has included, but by no means has been limited to, imperialism, concepts and constructions of the body, gender, politics, nationalism/internationalism and much more.

'Athleticism: A Case-Study of an Educational Ideology', a chapter in Brian Simon and Ian Bradley's *The Victorian Public School* (1975), set the stage for his acclaimed *Athleticism in the Victorian and Edwardian Public School: The Emergence and Consolidation of an Educational Ideology* (1981).[3] (An expanded second edition, which is briefly discussed at the conclusion of this contribution, was published by Cass in 2000.)

Reviewers were glowing in their praise. John Rae, in a three-page account in the *Times Literary Supplement*, declared that it was 'unlikely that this piece of English social history will receive a more perceptive and balanced treatment'.[4] Jeffrey Richards's article in *The Listener* described the book as awesomely scholarly and meticulously documented and pointed to the author's scrupulous analyses of 'the structure of symbolism and ritual that sustained the games-playing ideology'.[5] German sports historian Joachim K. Ruhl's assertion that *Athleticism in the Victorian and Edwardian Public School* 'set a terrifyingly high standard of scholarship in the young field of sports history in Britain' was matched by the evaluation of others. According to Ruhl, there had 'not been any sports historical investigation to match it on the Continent in the past decade'.[6] In life there are many paradoxes. One of the consequences of the 'terrifyingly high standard' set by his first sport history book was that Tony Mangan subsequently often was given little leeway for anything that reviewers did not conclude rose to its standard regardless of the fact that his growing contributions have led to new and highly promising lines of investigation that blazed new trails for others to tread.

In his review of *Athleticism and the Victorian and Edwardian Public School* William A. Freeman asked: 'How does a reviewer describe a milestone book in its field? ... No department of sport studies or physical education should fail to have it in its library and in use. ... I do not think I can overrate the value of Mangan's contribution to sport studies'. Freeman cited the thoroughness of the study, the author's analytic acumen, and his abilities to put 'practices and theory into the context of the time, rather than simply judging it against a constantly-changing modern scene'. Gerald Redmond's equally laudatory review in the December 1982 *Canadian Journal of History of Sport* pointed out that the *New Statesman* as well as *The Listener* and the *Times Literary Supplement* had all given it glowing accounts. When a new book on what had been considered a fairly familiar subject elicited three pages of text and a front cover illustration of a cricket match between Eton and Harrow upon which the words 'Sport and the Public Schools' were inscribed, Redmond wrote, 'it is obvious that a publication of some significance has emerged'. Summarizing the book's several qualities, he pointed to the author's 'conscientious review of related literature combined with appropriate use of primary and secondary sources, genuinely original hypotheses ... distinctive prose (with often an exquisite turn of phrase)' – an accolade that many other reviewers also would note – and judicious selection of a cross-section of six British public schools to achieve an 'in-depth analysis of their similarities and differences with regard to the prevailing Athleticism'.[7]

The *American Historical Review*, likewise, noted the merits of examining six representative schools from six distinct classes of institutions, as did Patrick Scott in a review for *Victorian Studies*. Scott found the book to be 'surprisingly fresh in its approach' to what might appear, on first glance, to be 'well-tilled fields' – and made two passing observations that deserve more thoughtful treatment than typically has been accorded such matters: first, the book's final two chapters reflected a shift from a 'social-historical to a more anthropological approach'; second, the author had come to his study 'as an expert in physical education' – which was correct, but only in part.

With regard to the first observation, sport is a highly symbolic and symbol-laden cultural construct; hence a knowledge of anthropology can be of considerable value for historians and other social scientists who seek to probe its many ritual, festival and other symbolic 'frames'.[8] With regard to the second, there has been, and still is, a tendency in the academic world to view those who have earned one or more of their degrees and/or worked in physical education as being less qualified than others to produce sound scholarly work in spite of the fact that several such individuals have brought forth excellent studies that have important insights to contribute to social and cultural history. It is quite possible – more likely probable – that individuals so trained bring insights to their topics that others do not possess. The value of 'the insider's' (*emic*) as well as 'the outsider's' (*etic*) 'view' has been demonstrated in a range of historical writings, including those about medicine.[9] In fact, the importance of both perspectives was made many years ago by Maurice Mandelbaum in *The Anatomy of Historical*

Knowledge (1977).[10] And more than three decades ago Peter McIntosh noted the value of biological as well as social science knowledge in the historical study of both sport and physical education.[11]

The fact is that Tony Mangan's academic training in social anthropology, sociology and social history has provided him with a unique assemblage of scholarly abilities that he has put to use in the many works that he has produced.

He graduated from Durham University in 1961 with a BA honours degree in social anthropology. He then enrolled at Loughborough College, where his main subjects were education and physical education. Later he obtained a higher education qualification at Oxford University in the sociology of education, and subsequently obtained a doctorate in social history at Glasgow University. Publications informed by the perspectives of all these disciplines may be found in his contributions to the literature.

The antecedents for Tony Mangan's 'eagerly awaited'[12] second book, *The Games Ethic and Imperialism: Aspects of the Diffusion of an Ideal* (1986), are to be found in articles like 'Eton in India: The Imperial Diffusion of a Victorian Education Ethic', published in *History of Education* in 1978, and 'Almond of Loretteo: Educational Rebel, Reformer and Visionary', which appeared in *Scottish Education Studies* the following year. Writing for *Victorian Studies*, the reviewer John Galbraith described *The Games Ethic and Imperialism* as an 'entertaining narrative' that was a 'delight to read' and a work that was likely to have 'wide appeal'. A similar view was expressed by Alan Metcalfe, who commented on the author's 'brilliance of writing' and 'penetrating insights' into a ideology that extended to Sudan, Nigeria, India, Canada and beyond but also expressed concern that its chapters were unevenly 'rooted in primary sources'. Such a criticism merits respect, of course; but it is important to remind ourselves that the historian is constrained by the sources that can be located. Moreover, at the time that *The Games Ethic and Imperialism* appeared, there had been few studies that sought to investigate the diffusion of these ideologies beyond the English-speaking world. (Fortunately, this fascinating phenomenon has been receiving growing attention, largely, it would appear, due to Mangan's continuing leadership.) Phyllis Martin concluded her review of *The Games Ethic* in the *American Historical Review* with a significant sentence: 'With this stimulating work of Mangan, new directions for further research have been pointed out.'[13] Indeed, his continuing efforts to open up new vistas and his ability to locate possibilities for further research in an expanding number of cultural settings have benefited many other scholars.

The following years saw the publication of important volumes, often in emerging areas, that Tony Mangan was instrumental in conceptualizing, encouraging and moving to completion. One of these areas has been gender and the construction of icons in and around which gender roles have been articulated. In the preface to *Masculinities* (1995) R.W. Connell noted that it had been only in 'the last five years' that there had been an impressive growth of social science research in relation to 'masculinity'.[14] *Manliness and Morality: Middle Class Masculinity in Britain and America, 1800–1940* (edited by Mangan and James Walvin), which appeared in 1986, was one of the earliest efforts to explicitly use sports, exercise and kindred matters as an organizing focus for studies in the then developing area of men's history and masculinity.[15] It certainly was one of the first – if not the first – to explore these matters in a transatlantic context. According to Sheldon Rothblatt, the collection demonstrated how 'truly interesting' the subject could be 'as alert minds push in all directions to capture and explain society's endless fascination with sex-linked character traits, their possible meanings, forms, and purposes'.[16]

From 'Fair Sex' to Feminism: Sport and the Socialization of Women in the Industrial and Post-Industrial Eras (edited by Mangan and Roberta J. Park and soon to be reprinted) also had a transatlantic dimension, and was formed around papers delivered at the 1984 British Society for Sport History conference and published as the May 1985 volume of *The British Journal of Sports History*. The reviewer Jean Barman concluded that the 'complexities of the various interpretations' offered by the dozen contributing scholars from three continents provided insights that were 'far more challenging and provocative than would have been any single perspective' and that the volume merited serious consideration by social historians as well as by historians of sport. Nancy Bouchier cited its 'focus on analysis, rather than description' and the incorporation of insights from recent developments in social history and women's history as being among this collection's strengths and noted that the clear introduction gave the book 'a cohesiveness many essay collections lack'.[17] (Certain antecedents for this may be located in a series of stimulating discussions and meetings during the early 1980s while Tony was serving as an acting professor at the University of California,

Berkeley, and as a research associate at the university's prestigious
Center for Studies in Higher Education.)

   Sport in Africa: Essays in Social History (with William J.
Baker) drew together 12 essays by anthropologists, sociologists, historians, political
scientists and educationists (both editors contributed chapters) whose
essays were intended to help bring about a meaningful revision of the
traditional 'imperialist view of African history'.[18] Since previous
discussions of sport in Africa had 'been pre-occupied with South Africa
and the issue of apartheid', the reviewer John Corlett observed, the more
broadly conceived *Sport in Africa* was an especially welcome addition –
one that could 'be recommended most highly to anyone with either an
academic or a general interest in the topic'. Corlett found much to
commend, although he regretted the absence of chapters dealing with
the French, Belgian and Portuguese colonial influence; but he
acknowledged that the editors had attempted (apparently
unsuccessfully) to recruit such contributions and that in some of the
countries only a 'limited number of scholarly sources' were available.[19]
(Scholars will be pleased to learn that many of the omissions due to lack
of available materials in the 1980s will be rectified in a forthcoming
volume edited by Tony Mangan, entitled *Sport in Africa: Nationalism,
Globalization, Commercialism.*)

   Arguably, several of Mangan's subsequent volumes could be
criticized for not being sufficiently comprehensive. It is essential to ask
what an editor is to do when papers dealing with topics that he would
like to include cannot be secured: wait until they become available –
which may be a very long time, if at all – or publish a volume whose
contents may serve as a stimulus for others to conceptualize and pursue
further investigations? The latter seems by far the more logical and
intellectually productive approach. Joseph Arbena's review of *Sport in
Africa*, which praised the anthology's originality, underscores this point,
making the cogent observation that because historians and other scholars
of sport tended to be 'concentrated in those metropolitan countries
where they research primarily their own sporting cultures' many
societies (to date) had produced 'few academic students of sport'. More
global understandings of 'the place of games, sports, recreation, and
leisure in individual and societal behavior', Arbena continued, must
await 'a vast amount of research and analysis'.[20] We are coming
considerably closer to that 'vast amount of research and analysis' thanks
to the work of Mangan and his co-contributors. What Tony Mangan has

written recently in *Sport in Asian Society: Past and Present* is as pertinent to the past as to the present contributions from his exploratory pen: 'Asia then is the focus of this innovatory volume. ... The state of present research and the space available means that this volume cannot be satisfactorily comprehensive, but it attempts to be stimulatingly exploratory.'

With relevant modifications, Arbena's observations about the need for research and analyses that might open the way to more global understanding of sport – and cognate areas such as leisure and physical education – are applicable to 'metropolitan countries' as well. Language can be a severe barrier to sharing knowledge and understandings; and reading ability in a language other than one's own in no way ensures that one can grasp the nuances – even the essential elements – of writings produced by members of another culture. Jean-François Loudcher, Christian Vivier and André Gounot's recent article 'French Sports Historiography: Institutional Aspects', published in *Stadion* in 2001, presents a compelling instance of how culture, institutional differences and historical traditions shape the ways in which historians choose and conceptualize their topics and go about investigating them. The authors' opening sentence should be attended to with thoughtful consideration: 'French sport historiography (understood here in its widest sense) shows a different picture when compared to the Anglo–Saxon countries, in both its topics and methods on the one hand and in its institutionalization on the other'. Their closing sentences are no less important and also are applicable more broadly: 'French sport history has an urgent need to develop international exchanges ... to show its rich and original content to the scientific world ... [and] enrich itself by the confrontation with foreign models which will further widen its scientific and international scope.'[21]

How are such international exchanges to be obtained? This is a question well worth considering. Electronic networks are becoming increasingly popular, and in a number of ways intellectually profitable (although they remain – at least for some of us – a little too impersonal and lacking in context). Conferences and congresses that are attended by scholars from different countries and diverse cultures are another possibility. In recent years these have been increasing as more national and regional sport history societies have been organized. For those who do not have the time, resources or inclination to travel abroad, the International Society for the History of Sport and Physical Education

(ISHPES), formed in 1989 by a merger of the International Association for the History of Physical Education and Sport (HISPA, founded in 1973) and the International Committee on the History of Physical Education and Sport (ICOSH, founded in 1967),[22] has produced proceedings of papers delivered at its biennial congresses and seminars. (Since 1993, several of these have been published by Academia Verlag.)

The proceedings of the First European Seminar of the Committee on European Sport History (established in 1993) were published in 1997.[23] Other research groups also have been formed. The reasons for the creation of these, as has been noted, have been several;[24] and something akin to a 'medieval feast'[25] has become possible for those who are able – and willing – to gain access to the ever growing number of publications.

Important insights can be gleaned from consulting proceedings, but the number of pages allowed each author is usually small and the quality of their contents tends to be uneven. Moreover, university libraries often are unwilling to subscribe to them; hence, knowledge of their existence is limited. Proceedings also do not have the same academic cachet as do refereed journals. Academic journals (to which libraries are more inclined to subscribe and the best of which, at least, have more exacting standards of scholarship) are essential for disseminating findings, stimulating ideas and advancing research.

With regard to sport history, important ground was broken in the 1970s with the appearance of the *Canadian Journal of History of Sport and Physical Education* (1970), which became *Sport History Review* in 1996.[26] The *Journal of Sport History*, created by the North American Society for Sport History, published its first issue in 1974. (Both journals have expressed interest in articles whose appeal is relevant to an international audience, but their editorial boards remain largely English-speaking.)[27] The first issue of the German-based *Stadion: Internationale Zeitschrift für Geschichte des Sport* appeared in 1975.

The 1980s witnessed a welcome growth with the initiation of publications like The Australian Society for Sports History's *Sporting Traditions* and *Sport-Histoire: Revue Internationale des Sports et des Jeux*.[28] The *British Journal of Sports History*, launched as an independent but associated journal of the then recently established British Society of Sports History (Mangan was a founding member of BSSH and its first chair), issued its first volume in 1984 with the stated desire of stimulating, promoting, and coordinating 'interest in the history of sport, recreation, and leisure, with special, but not exclusive reference to the British Isles'.[29] Three years later the *BJSH* informed readers that its name had been changed to *The International Journal of the History of Sport*. The original 13-member editorial board was expanded to 24. An executive editor (in addition to three editors); regional editors for Australasia, Canada, Western Europe, Eastern Europe and the USSR, Japan, Latin America and the USA; and editors for women, society, sport, English language and foreign languages and bibliographic editors were announced.[30] *Sport-Histoire* called the change a '*heureuse initiative*' and expressed hope that the more international editorial board would lead to an awareness of the work of 'researchers in sport history from the four corners of the world'.[31]

With Tony Mangan at the helm as executive editor, the newly renamed and restructured *IJHS* began to move more explicitly toward the international dimension articulated in its May 1987 preface: 'It is hoped that in the future academics from all over the world will contribute to expanding the body of knowledge on sport, leisure and recreation through [its] pages'. By May 1990 the *IJHS*, which may be considered the leading international journal dealing with the evolution of that fascinating phenomenon 'sport', had published articles and/or commentaries – as well as book reviews – about sport and related topics in Japan, Scandinavia, the Philippines, China, Germany, West Africa, Malaysia, India, South America and an ever-widening sphere.

The new executive academic editor's dedication to more international work also was reflected in the growing number of books that he would edit. The wide-ranging *Pleasure, Profit, Proselytism: British Culture and Sport at Home and Abroad* (1988), which appears to have been stimulated – at least in part – by Eric Hobsbawm's recognition of the importance of sport in the creation of politically and social cohesive 'invented traditions',[32] included chapters dealing with Australia, Canada, South Africa and the West Indies. Keith Sandiford found it to be 'a fine anthology' even though Pakistan, India and New Zealand were not included.[33] Subsequent volumes such as *Sport in Australasian Society: Past and Present* (co-edited with John Nauright) and *Sport in Asian Society: Past and Present* (co-edited with Fan Hong) now have greatly expanded and extended the scope of the earlier volumes.

Regarding *Pleasure, Profit, Proselytism*, Peter Bilsborough stated that while a more 'complex integrated picture' of British contributions to imperial patterns might have been achieved in a book written by a single author, the preparation of such a work could take 'a lifetime'; hence, Mangan was to be congratulated for developing a fine collection that truly could be read with 'pleasure and profit'.[34]

Mangan's main interest has always been socialization. *The Imperial Curriculum*, which evolved from a 1986 meeting of the International Standing Conference for History of Education, explored aspects of the construction of 'racial images and education in the British colonial experience' in ten countries.[35] *'Benefits Bestowed'?: Education and British Imperialism* (1988), a contribution to the Manchester University Press 'Studies in Imperialism' series, focused on educational policies and programmes in England and various parts of the British Empire. A *Sporting Traditions* reviewer credited the book's 'refreshingly new viewpoints'. A reviewer in *Victorian Studies* complained of a lack of cohesiveness because the editor had allowed authors to choose 'their own topics and periods of study' and ask 'their own questions', yet agreed that the anthology had 'raised a great many questions' that warranted further consideration.[36] A scrupulous respect for eclecticism has characterized all of Mangan's collections. This approach self-evidently offers opportunities for greater originality. In its companion volume, *Making Imperial Mentalities: Socialisation and British Imperialism* (1990), Mangan's training in anthropology was evidenced by his interest in examining how the processes of *enculturation* (aggressive induction into the dominant culture) and *acculturation* (a more passive absorption of elements of that culture) operated in attempts that were made to ensure that individuals and groups within both the dominant and subordinate cultures in the British Empire learned values, attitudes and behaviours that would 'ensure the survival of the imperial system'.[37] (Contributions from scholars with specialties in education, history and political science were included.) Aspects of both these works were extended in *A Significant Social Revolution: Cross-Cultural Aspects of the Evolution of Compulsory Education* (1994).[38]

The ability to formulate significant research questions is of no small consequence in scholarship. Also important is the ability to recognize contemporary concerns and to fashion studies that will address these. A careful review of Tony Mangan's published works shows both careful and insightful planning and a penetrating ability to 'seize the moment'. In *The Cultural Bond: Sport, Empire, Society* (1992), he again underscored the need for deeper historical, anthropological, and sociological understandings of sport. The book's focus is imperial sport as a moral metaphor and political symbol that proved to be extremely useful in forming a 'cultural bond' within empire and dominion. Harold Perkin's observation in the Epilogue is especially striking and is well worth considering in the light of events such as the second international conference of the International Society for the Study of European Ideas held at the Catholic University, Leuven, in 1990. Perkin wrote: 'Thus it [sport] helped the Empire to decolonize on a friendlier basis than any other in the world's history, and so contributed to the transformation of the British Empire into the Commonwealth of Nations'.[39] The focus of the Leuven conference – 'Towards a Future Europe: A Comparative History of European Nationalism' – was directed to how 'a new European political, cultural and social consciousness' might be forged. *Tribal Identities: Nationalism, Europe, Sport* (1996; republished in 2002), which first appeared as a special issue of the *IJSH*, evolved from a session at this conference that Tony Mangan had organized.[40]

The need for heroes, Roy Browne and Marshall Fishwick have written in *The Hero in Transition* (1983), 'is inherent in human history'.[41] During the last century the icon of 'the sporting hero' who serves collective national ends has gained increasing ascendancy. *European Heroes: Myth, Identity, Sport* (co-edited by Richard Holt, J.A. Mangan and Pierre Lanfranchi, 1996) explored symbolic meanings that have been attached to such individuals. The volume grew out of seminars directed at promoting the idea of a 'People's Europe' that had been held at the Centre for European Culture at the European University Institute in Florence in the early 1990s. Its prologue contains the arresting observation: 'Arguably Europe now needs ... unifying heroes and it is perhaps preferable they come from future gamesfields rather than past battlefields'.[42]

The muscular male body as 'moral symbol' and masculinity as a metaphor are explored in *Shaping the Superman* (1999) and its companion volume *Superman Supreme* (2000), both of which are concerned with the 'Facist Body as Political Icon'. Whereas the former explores the male body as 'a pre-eminent symbol of invulnerability, aggression and power' incorporated in the 'Aryan man' and the 'Nazis' cult of Nordic manhood', the latter extends such examinations more globally to Spain, Bulgaria, South America, China, Japan and other parts of the world. The importance of gaining deeper understanding of this phenomenon is underscored in the editor's striking introductory observation that certain neo-fascist tendencies embodied in male icons seem to be re-emerging in various countries.[43]

Words have meanings and the contexts in which they are used is of no small importance. This point is illustrated by *The Nordic World* (1998), which includes chapters dealing with the development of sport and gymnastics in Norway, Sweden, Denmark and Finland. In his Introduction, co-editor Henrik Meinander asks the pertinent question 'What should actually be included in the all-embracing concept of *Norden* – the Nordic nations?' – pointing out that in the eighteenth century the whole of Russia, northern Germany and certain regions of the Arctic Ocean had been included.[44] Its interesting chapters address a number of topics that too few sport historians outside Scandinavia have known much about. *Sport in Australasian Society*, which coincided with the 2000 Sydney Olympics and explored the political, social and aesthetic influences of modern sport in New Zealand and Australia, was based on a special issue of *IJSH*.[45]

Other recent volumes offer new information and insights regarding the search for emancipation in and through 'freeing the body' as articulated by selected women in Western and Eastern cultures (*Freeing the Female Body*, co-edited with Fan Hong);[46] and the emergence, evolution and diffusion of sports in Latin America (*Sport in Latin American Society*, co-edited with Lamartine DaCosta).[47] All are welcome additions to the ever-widening sphere of sport history.

Additional vistas were opened by the creation of *The European Sports History Review*, launched in 1999 with Tony Mangan as executive academic editor and a 12-member editorial board representing ten European countries. Its annual publications have included: *Sport in Europe: Politics, Class, Gender* (1999); *Making European Masculinities* (2000); and *Europe, Sport, World: Shaping Global Societies* (2001), which includes selected aspects of developments in Brazil, Japan, Singapore, Palestine, Cuba and elsewhere beyond Europe. Volume 4, *Middle-Class Revolutionaries* (2002) addresses a theme that Mangan set forth in the prologue to the first volume of *ESHR* when discussing the relevance of Peter Gay's *The Bourgeois Experience: Victoria to Freud* (1984) for historians of sport – namely the need for more systematic and detailed concentrations on middle-class culture.[48] *A Sport-Loving Society: Victorian and Edwardian Middle-Class England at Play* and *Disreputable Pleasures: Less Virtuous Victorians at Play* (co-edited with Mike Huggins), both forthcoming, are expected to contribute to such studies and to stimulate others.

His far-ranging efforts and achievements have brought James A. Mangan numerous honours and recognitions. He has been named a fellow of the Royal Historical Society, a fellow of the Royal Anthropological Institute and a corresponding fellow of the American Academy of Kinesiology and Physical Education – an aggregation that reflects his broad academic and professional training. He has received invitations to lecture and speak in Africa, North and South America, Asia, Australasia and Europe. As a Research Associate and/or Visiting Scholar/Professor, he has been associated with the universities of California and Alberta, and with Oxford and Cambridge. He established, and served as director of, the International Research Centre for Sport, Socialisation and Society at De Montfort University (Bedford). In addition to initiating the Manchester University Press 'International Studies in the History of Sport' series, in 1997, he created and serves as series editor for the Frank Cass 'Sport in the Global Society' series, which now includes more than 50 volumes. In 1999 he initiated *Culture, Sport, Society*, the first international interdisciplinary journal to deal with these topics (e.g. anthropology, sociology, political science, social history), with the objective of developing new approaches to the study of sport. The recently inaugurated journal *Soccer and Society* (with Tony Mangan as executive academic editor) is the first international journal devoted to the world's most popular game. While doing all this, he has continued to produce lively, informative and valuable articles on a wide array of topics. On 27 November 2001, a revised edition of his acclaimed *Athleticism in the Victorian and Edwardian Public School* and seven of his other books were launched at the Jubilee Room, Houses of Parliament.[49] In addition, he has presented, with Frank Galligan, 'Student Sports Studies' as a new series intended to meet the needs of students in high schools and institutions of higher learning in Europe, Britain and the rest of the English-speaking world.

One final point may be made with emphasis. Invariably, Tony Mangan's work is always a pleasure to read: clear, flowing, elegant. I recently came across Sir Roy Strong's comment on C.V. Wedgwood's famous *The King's Peace*: 'history as I wanted to write it: clear, accessible, captivating'. It will do for my comment on Tony Mangan's style. Incidentally, another associated quality should never be forgotten. He once said to me that for over 20 years he had rewritten the world. His editorial capacity to bring many academics from many parts of the world to publication standard in English is an unsung but major part of his contribution to the history of sport.

In the two decades since *Athleticism* first appeared the social history of sport has greatly matured. As was said near the beginning of this article, Tony Mangan has had a great deal to do with its scholarly emergence, contributing unrelentingly his own articles, chapters and monographs, an ever-expanding series of exciting edited works, and spurring scholars from around the world to research, write and publish fascinating, important and 'downright good' history. Forthcoming collections such as *Militarism, Sport, Europe: War Without Weapons* – the next volume of *The European Sports History Review* – *Ethnicity, Sport, Identity: Struggles for Status* (with Andrew Ritchie) and *Soccer, Women, Sexual Liberation: Kicking Off a New Era* (with Fan Hong) and two co-authored monographs: *Soccer Schoolmasters: Pioneering the People's Game Across the Globe* (with Colm Hickey) and *Blooding the Male: Masculinity, Sport, Hunting* (with Callum McKenzie) promise even more.[50] In the Foreword and Introduction to the new edition of *Athleticism in the Victorian and Edwardian Public School*, the work that launched all this, two distinguished cultural historians – Sheldon Rothblatt and Jeffrey Richards – rightly credit that now 'classic work' with launching a new generation of scholarly writing. 'Not since Edward C. Mack of Columbia University produced his extraordinary studies of the English public school in the 1930s,' Rothblatt wrote, 'had there been a work so interesting.'[51] Jeffrey Richards concludes his Introduction with the observation of the importance of the new Frank Cass edition to the 'necessary and important task of adequately recording an essentially English middle-class contribution, both directly and indirectly, to British, imperial, commonwealth and global culture'.[52] Given his record to date, we can look forward confidently to ever more stimulating and illuminating works produced by James A. (Tony) Mangan!

NOTES

1. Leonard Koppett, 'Introduction', in Paul D. Staudohar and James A. Mangan (eds), *The Business of Professional Sports* (Urbana, IL: University of Illinois Press, 1991), pp.ix–xi.
2. J.A. Mangan, 'Series Editor's Foreword', in Stephen G. Jones, *Sport, Politics, and the Working Class: Organized Labour and Sport in Inter-War Britain* (Manchester: Manchester University Press, 1988), p.vi.
3. In the opening paragraph of 'Walking in the Footsteps of a Pioneer: Peter McIntosh – Trail Blazer in the History of Sport', *The International Journal of the History of Sport*, 18, 2 (2001), 136–47, Mike Huggins points to the influence of McIntosh's work on this highly received study.
4. John Rae, 'Play Up, Play Up', *Times Literary Supplement*, 2 Oct. 1981, 1120–2.
5. Jeffrey Richards, 'Playing the Game', *The Listener*, 6 May 1982, 16–17.

6. Joachim K. Ruhl, review of *Athleticism in the Victorian and Edwardian Public School*, The *British Journal of Sports History*, 1, 1 (1984), 90–5.

7. Gerald Redmond, review of *Athleticism in the Victorian and Edwardian Public School, Canadian Journal of History of Sport*, 8, 2 (1982), 80–2.

8. See especially John J. MacAloon, 'Olympic Games and the Theory of Spectacle in Modern Societies', in John J. MacAloon (ed.), *Rite, Drama, Festival, Spectacle: Rehearsals Toward a Theory of Cultural Performance* (Philadelphia, PA: Institute for the Study of Human Issues, 1984), pp.241–80.

9. For example, in his review of W. Bruce Fye's *American Cardiology: The History of a Specialty and Its College* (Baltimore, MD, and London: Johns Hopkins University Press, 1996), Steven J. Peitzman has pointed to the merits of a history 'written by someone within the specialty who also commands historiographic expertise': *Journal of the History of Medicine*, 52, 4 (1997), 509–10. A medical doctor, Fye has been chairman of the department of cardiology at Marshfield Clinic, Marshfield, Wisconsin as well as professor of the history of medicine at the University of Wisconsin.

10. Maurice Mandelbaum, *The Anatomy of Historical Knowledge* (Baltimore, MD: Johns Hopkins University Press, 1977), 11-13.

11. Peter C. McIntosh, 'What Is History of Sport and Physical Education?', *Canadian Journal of History of Sport and Physical Education*, 1, 1 (1970), i–ii. There is a paucity of studies that take this admonition into account. Among the valuable models that might be cited is the extensive work of Patricia Vertinsky such as her widely known *The Eternally Wounded Woman: Women, Doctors and Exercise in the Late Nineteenth Century* (Manchester: Manchester University Press, 1990) and John Hoberman, *Mortal Engines: The Science of Performance and the Dehumanization of Sport* (New York: Free Press, 1992).

12. Alan Metcalfe, review of *The Games Ethic and Imperialism, Canadian Journal of History of Sport*, 18, 1 (May 1987), 105.

13. Phyllis A. Martin, review of *The Games Ethic and Imperialism, American Historical Review*, 92, 2 (1987), 385–6.

14. R.W. Connell, *Masculinities* (Berkeley and Los Angeles, CA: University of California Press, 1995), p.ix. One could argue, of course, that all studies of men and sport are in some way studies of masculinity.

15. J.A. Mangan and James Walvin, (eds.), *Manliness and Morality: Middle-Class Masculinity in Britain and America, 1800-1940* (Manchester: Manchester University Press, 1987), 1-4.

16. Sheldon Rothblatt, review of *Manliness and Morality, The International Journal of the History of Sport*, 6,1 (1989), 142–4.

17. Jean Barman, review of *From 'Fair Sex' to Feminism, The International Journal of the History of Sport*, 5, 1 (1988), 143–5; Nancy B. Bouchier, review of *From 'Fair Sex' to Feminism, Canadian Journal of History of Sport*, 19, 2 (1988), 101–2.

18. William J. Baker and James A. Mangan, 'Introduction', in William J. Baker and James A. Mangan (eds), *Sport in Africa: Essays in Social History* (New York and London: Africana Publishing Co., 1987), p.vii.

19. John T. Corlett, review of *Sport in Africa, Canadian Journal of History of Sport*, 19, 2 (1988), 102–4.

20. Joseph L. Arbena, review of *Sport in Africa, Journal of Sport History*, 15, 2 (1988), 179–81.

21. Jean-Francois Loudcher, Christian Vivier and Andre Gounot, 'French Sports Historiography: Institutional Aspects', *Stadion*, 27 (2001), 7–21.

22. Steve Bailey, *Science in the Service of Physical Education and Sport: The Story of the International Council of Sport Science and Physical Education, 1956–1996* (Chichester: John Wiley and Sons, 1996) discusses ideological differences and other matters that divided ICOSH and HISPA for many years.

23. Arnd Kruger and Anjela Teja (eds.), *La Comune Eredità dello Sport in Europe: Atti del i Seminario Europeo di Storia dello Sport* (Rome: Scuolo dello Sport – CONI, 1997).

24. The point is pertinently made in 'Walking in the Footsteps of a Pioneer'.

25. The amount and range of such foodstuffs has been ably discussed in J.C. Drummond and A. Wilbraham, *The Englishman's Food: A History of Five Centuries of English Diet* (London: Jonathan Cape, 1939).

26. Don Morrow, 'Canadian Journal of History of Sport', *ISHPES Bulletin*, 11 (July 1996), 14–15.
27. 'Editorial', *Journal of Sport History*, 1, 1 (1974), 1–2; 'Editorial Statement', *Sport History Review*, 29, 1 (1998).
28. Regrettably, due to financial exigencies *Sport-Histoire* ceased publication after four issues. Other initiatives that have been launched are discussed by Thierry Terret, 'Pourquoi n'y a-t-il ni société française d'histoire de sport en France, ni revue française d'histoire du sport'?, *ISHPES Bulletin*, 22 (December 2001), 26–8.
29. 'Statement from the Editors', *The British Journal of the History of Sport*, 1, 1 (1984), 3. Indeed, the British Society of Sport History's October 1983 *Newsletter* (4) already had reflected that organization's interest in forging links with 'scholars in the field all round the globe' and an interdisciplinary approach that would attract anthropologists, sociologists, and others.
30. 'Editor's Preface', *The International Journal of the History of Sport*, 4, 1 (1987), 2.
31. Review of *The International Journal of the History of Sport*, *Sport/Histoire: Revue Internationale des Sports et des Jeux*, 2 (1988).
32. J.A. Mangan (ed.), 'Introduction', *Pleasure, Profit, Proselytism: British Culture and Sport at Home and Abroad, 1700–1914* (London: Frank Cass, 1988), 1–3; Eric Hobsbawm and Terence Ranger (eds), *The Invention of Tradition* (Cambridge: Cambridge University Press, 1983).
33. Keith A.P. Sandiford, review of *Pleasure, Profit, Proselytism*, *Sporting Traditions*, 6, 1 (1989), 104–8.
34. Peter Bilsborough, review of *Pleasure, Profit, Proselytism*, *The International Journal of the History of Sport*, 7, 1 (1990), 152–3.
35. J.A. Mangan (ed.), *The Imperial Curriculum: Racial Images and Education in the British Colonial Experience* (London: Routledge, 1991).
36. Katharine Moore, review of *'Benefits Bestowed'?*, *Sporting Traditions*, 7, 2 (1991), 220–2; Kinley Brauer, review of *Benefits Bestowed?*, *Victorian Studies*, 34, 1 (1990), 124–5. Edited works frequently elicit such criticisms as, for example, David H. Galaty's review of William Coleman and Frederick L. Holmes (eds), *The Investigative Enterprise: Experimental Physiology in Nineteenth Century Medicine* (Berkeley, CA: University of California Press, 1988), *Journal of the History of Medicine*, 44, 4 (1989), 524–5.
37. J.A. Mangan (ed.), 'Introduction', *Making Imperial Mentalities: Socialisation and British Imperialism* (Manchester: Manchester University Press, 1990), 3.
38. J.A. Mangan (ed.), *A Significant Social Revolution: Cross-Cultural Aspects of the Evolution of Compulsory Education* (London and Portland, OR: The Woburn Press, 1994).
39. Harold Perkin, 'Teaching the Nations How to Play: Sport and Society in the British Empire and Commonwealth', in J.A. Mangan (ed.), *The Cultural Bond: Sport, Empire, Society* (London: Frank Cass, 1992), p.211.
40. J.A. Mangan (ed.), *Tribal Identities: Nationalism, Europe, Sport* (London and Portland, OR: Frank Cass Publishers, 1996).
41. Roy B. Browne and Marshall W. Fishwick, *The Hero in Transition* (Bowling Green, OH: Bowling Green University Popular Press, 1983), p.9.
42. Richard Holt, J.A. Mangan and Pierre Lanfranchi (eds), *European Heroes: Myth, Identity, Sport* (London and Portland, OR: Frank Cass, 1996), p.3 (originally published as *The International Journal of the History of Sport*, 13, 1 (1996)).
43. J.A. Mangan (ed.), *Shaping the Superman: Fascist Body as Political Icon – Aryan Fascism* (London and Portland, OR: Frank Cass, 1999); J.A. Mangan (ed.), *Superman Supreme: Fascist Body as Political Icon – Global Fascism* (London and Portland, OR: Frank Cass, 2000), pp.231–2.
44. Henrik Meinander, 'Introduction', in Henrik Meinander and J.A. Mangan (eds), *The Nordic World: Sport in Society* (London and Portland, OR: Frank Cass, 1998), p.2.
45. J.A. Mangan and John Nauright (eds), *Sport in Australasian Society: Past and Present* (London and Portland, OR: Frank Cass, 2000).
46. J.A. Mangan and Fan Hong (eds), *Freeing the Female Body: Inspirational Icons* (London and Portland, OR: Frank Cass, 2001).
47. J.A. Mangan and Lamartine P. DaCosta (eds), *Sport in Latin American Society: Past and Present* (London and Portland, OR: Frank Cass, 2001).

48. J.A. Mangan (ed.), *Sport in Europe: Politics, Class, Gender: The European Sports History Review*, 1 (London and Portland: Frank Cass, 1999), pp.vii–ix.
49. 'The Study of Sport and Its Increasing Importance', *Prism*, 184 (November 2001), 3.
50. See J.A. Mangan 'Prologue – Asian Sport: From the Recent Past' in J.A. Mangan and Fan Hong (eds), *Sport in Asian Society: Past and Present* (London: Frank Cass, 2002), pp. 17–18.
51. Sheldon Rothblatt, 'Foreword', *Athleticism in the Victorian and Edwardian Public School: The Emergence and Consolidation of an Educational Ideology* (London and Portland, OR: Frank Cass, 2000), p.xviii.
52. Jeffrey Richards, 'Introduction to the New Edition', *Athleticism in the Victorian and Edwardian Public School*, p.xlix.

4

Direct and Indirect Influence: J.A. Mangan and the Victorian Middle Classes: Major Revisionist in the History of Sport

MIKE HUGGINS

British historians have always been preoccupied by class, and in the last 30 years occasionally almost uniquely obsessed to a point that is puzzling to colleagues in Europe, the Americas and elsewhere. Social 'class', usually but not always in its loose, vernacular sense, has become 'the dominant paradigm in the study of British sport', the cardinal explanatory concept 'which has shaped its discourse' and 'steered its discussion'.[1] When in the 1970s the analysis of class and social structure in nineteenth-century Britain became a favourite topic of research among social historians, the top-down methodologies and emphasis on the upper classes and ruling elites that earlier historians like Napier, Kitson Clark or Perkin had adopted were largely discontinued in favour of greater concern with the urban middle-class elites, the labour aristocracy and skilled workers. As part of this revisionary emphasis on social class and 'history from below', other 'new' social historians began to sketch out the details of how a rival middle-class network of social relationships emerged over the course of the nineteenth century to challenge earlier models of social relationships. Alongside this went a reconsideration with working-class experience, owing much to the initiatives of E.P. Thompson.

In the more specialized field of leisure and sport, one related major issue that attracted significant attention was the assessment of the effects of industrialization and ubanization on working-class culture, an issue first explored by Malcolmson.[2] A second issue concerned the extent and success of middle-class value systems intended to reduce social disorder and civilize the masses, well illustrated by Bailey's work on Victorian 'rational' recreations.[3] A third area of renewed interest and emphasis from the 1970s was on Victorian values, styles of life and ethical codes and ideals, much influenced by Marxist accounts of social control and cultural hegemony. New pictures of paternalism, patriarchy, Victorian individualism, values acting together and in part as new forms of social cohesion and 'respectability' in the middle and late Victorian period in contexts such as the factory, the family or the emerging commercial leisure activities began to be drawn. Most of these approaches were marked by a reluctance to research the leisure of the middle classes directly. The middle classes were discussed largely through their alleged powerful impact on working-class life, an approach dominated by concepts first of 'social control' and later of cultural 'hegemony'. Both concepts provided useful insights into working-class life and leisure, but were less useful in looking at middle-class leisure.

Concurrently, the historiography of Victorian schooling and education was subject to the same intensive ideological and reformist scrutiny, from a wide variety of perspectives, with Marxist writers like Brian Simon in the van.[4]

Enter J.A. Mangan. An edited collection on physical education and sport came out as early as 1973.[5] It drew on his training in social anthropology, sociology and social history, a combination almost certainly unique in the field of sports history, and one which positioned him well to develop the innovative new approaches to culture which still characterize his work. His subsequent monographs, collections and articles were all characterized by the meshing of sport with cultural values, attitudes and behaviour. His cardinal principle was that sport must be set within a cultural context and does not operate in a cultural vacuum. At the same time he recognized that sports in fact constituted a large, and increasing, part of culture and were at times (but not always) fissured along class lines.

It was, however, his outstanding *Athleticism in the Victorian and Edwardian Public School*, subtitled *The Emergence and Consolidation of an Educational Ideology*, published in 1981, that first marked him out as pre-eminent in his field, and which fused together understandings of class, culture and ideology in a study of the 'games cult' or 'athleticism'.[6] It has subsequently been designated as a classic, and among the most notable studies of culture, ideology and education. In a recent review I described it as a 'seminal' study which provided both a 'key to a proper understanding of the Victorian and Edwardian public school', and 'essential reading for those who seek to understand the ways in which the ideologies of athleticism and manliness shaped British national outlook'.[7]

There is a tendency to write about public schoolboys as an undifferentiated elite, and given the focus of this essay on the Victorian middle classes it may be necessary to remind some readers that the public schools varied in their intake and emphases – a point brought out superbly by Mangan in *Athleticism*. These schools were certainly not just for the upper classes. The vast majority had substantial numbers of middle-class pupils. They have even more today! Indeed, the public schools have been self-redesignated. They are mostly non-local, fee-paying, increasingly coeducational, predominantly boarding and as such they are mostly schools for the middle classes. Access is, and always was, largely, but not entirely, through the ability to pay. The nine most ancient, those investigated by the Clarendon Commission of 1864, such as Eton, Harrow, Rugby or Winchester, were probably patronized more than others by the upper classes, although these too certainly had many middle-class pupils. By contrast, despite the recommendations of the 1868 Taunton Commission that the middle classes should have only limited entry to public schools, proprietary boarding schools and grammar schools, many of the newer public schools already catered almost entirely for the middle-classes, mostly for the sons of those in professional careers.[8] These schools had been given a major boost by the spread of the railways, which made boarding schools accessible to a wider clientele. These 'burgeoning schools and colleges of the late Victorian middle classes' were of a variety of types.[9] Some were old endowed grammar schools such as Repton or Uppingham, some were newly endowed, such as Wellington (1859), others were joint-stock proprietary such as Cheltenham (1841) or Marlborough (1843). Others were sectarian establishments like Downside. Between 1837 and 1869 alone, some 31 boarding schools were founded, almost entirely for the sons of the middle class, while by 1868 there were also already some 791 endowed schools offering a somewhat higher than working-class education, and many middle-class boys went to local private schools.[10] Increasingly the public schools were a training ground in 'character', a preparation for imperial administrators, soldiers, entrepreneurs, mercenaries and teachers. The schools helped to diffuse public service ideals among the upper and middle classes. More importantly for British society, they were institutions for reconstructing illegitimate violence into legitimate violence and for inventing 'ways of exercising the hormonally challenged' – as Jeremy Paxman once memorably put it[11] – by means of games fields. The arguments for sport at these schools which supposedly bred 'character', were certainly complex. It is a notable virtue of Mangan's work that he makes this abundantly clear.

Mangan's work, of course, should not be seen in isolation. Peter McIntosh had stressed the role of the middle classes in schooling and sport, and gave a major boost to the cultural study of sport as long ago as the 1960s.[12] Explorations of manliness, athleticism and games in the public schools and universities, varying in emphasis, have been undertaken by distinguished writers such as Sheldon Rothblatt, Christopher Hibbert, David Newsome and notably E.C. Mack.[13] Mangan, of course, deals tellingly in his case studies of athleticism with resistance, its defeat and eventual impotence. And Dewey has usefully added to this story of resistance with his description of opposition, albeit limited, to the cult of athletics at Eton even during the time when athleticism was at its peak,[14] but as Mangan keeps on stressing, the story is by no means complete. Surprisingly a tendency to underemphasize the critical role of late Victorian and Edwardian middle-class schooling and education in period middle-class socialization is still discernible. Neil Tranter's book on sport, economy and society in Britain from 1750 to 1914, otherwise a readable, comprehensive introductory survey, has no reference to schools either in general or in particular in its index, and has only a very brief discussion of the role of public and grammar schools in the diffusion of athleticism.[15] An unfortunate omission.

Mangan's analysis of the rise of the games cult in the public schools and the part this eventually grew to play in the mindset of ruling elites in and beyond Britain as well as his necessary corrections of McIntosh, and his stress on the diversity of response to the cult, was critically important: vital for any understanding for the process of diffusion of the games ethic, although, of course, this process should be seen as only a partial explanation for the spread of modern sport – as Mangan makes clear in a recent chapter on the transmission of essentially English sport by the English middle classes to Argentina.[16] Athleticism, nevertheless, gave a major impetus to the first of the great sporting booms in the years after 1870, first in Britain and then beyond. Equally the public-school games ethic and the martial rhetoric of school magazines, sermons, speeches and lectures had a cumulative impact on the middle-class militarism of the late nineteenth and early twentieth centuries and the middle-class public-school games fields and imperial battlefields became increasingly linked.[17] Mangan has played a major revisionist role in bringing this to our notice.

Mangan immediately followed his work on public schools with studies of the impact of athleticism on grammar schools.[18] He then turned his attention to the 'ancient universities', at which late-Victorian undergraduates were encouraged to be active both in participating in and in disseminating sport. Oxford and Cambridge universities, which had been competing in cricket from 1827 and in rowing from 1829, increased their range of sports substantially from the 1850s onwards. Internal competition between colleges, especially at Cambridge, accentuated this trend. Mangan provided a first study of the sport of Victorian and Edwardian Cambridge as early as 1984, and has followed it up with further work on philathletic attitudes and behaviour at Oxford and Cambridge over the last two decades.[19] Both universities were highly important, although this stress on the 'old' universities has meant that the provincial university institutions of late Victorian England have as yet received too little attention. They introduced a somewhat more 'modern' curriculum, attracted a higher proportion of the industrial urban middle classes than did the older universities and seem to have taken up the 'games ethic' later in the diffusionist process. The one exception was Durham, where the Durham colleges were founding rowing clubs from the 1830s and 1840s thanks to the opportunities provided by the slow-flowing River Wear.

With the ball set in stimulating motion by Mangan, it is now time for others to kick it in the direction of the provincial universities. There could be fascinating findings. Lowerson has suggested that the provincial universities' slowness in taking up sport may be partly illusionary, since their students, living at home, may have often already turned for their sports to local associational groups and clubs by the time they became members of their student bodies.[20] This state of affairs could have been due to the fact that these new urban foundations usually lacked space and had to rent fields and premises. In short, Oxbridge set the tone. The red-bricks were keen to follow. As a result, the development of organized university sport came largely in and after the 1880s. Liverpool's athletic club and Manchester's Athletic Union were only formed in 1885. University College, London, had some athletics from the 1860s, but its athletics association was only formed in 1886, and it only acquired its own grounds in 1897. So what was their predominant sporting ethos over this period? What were the idealistic, utilitarian and social influences that shaped the lives of the students and lecturers in these later arrivals on the university scene? We simply do not know. We still lack the research.

Since the publication of *Athleticism*, Mangan has always been at the cutting edge of research, offering rich and pioneering perspectives on sport, and employing a highly readable, alliterative, allusive and invariably elegant writing style. Certainly the most prolific of culturally focused sports historians, his numerous authored and edited books have contributed high-quality cultural history to the field, most especially perhaps in his exploration of the relationship between middle classes, sport and morality. The major purpose of his Manchester University Press series, 'International Studies in the History of Sport', of course, was to set sport in its full cultural context, and its incorporation within conventional historical debates.

One of Mangan's outstanding abilities has been to recognize new and interesting areas which have been insufficiently developed, and which he has then gone on to explore. An example of this ability has been his probing of the association between middle-class education, sport and militarism as revealed in his edited collections, *Sport. Europe. Gender: Making European Masculinities* (2000) and *Tribal Identities: Nationalism, Europe and Sport* (1995), both for Frank Cass. His work has also included seminal publications on middle-class women and the ways in which they began to establish their own feminized sporting world, and were slowly admitted as closer companions to men in the burgeoning leisure forms emerging in the late nineteenth century. Closely following on the heels of Rubenstein's *Before the Suffragettes: Women's Emancipation in the 1890s*, which noted sport as one example of this emancipation, Mangan's and Park's innovatory collection *From Fair Sex to Feminism* (1987) focused much more tightly on the role of sport in the socialization of middle-class women.[21] Another later volume on the same lines which he initiated, was *Freeing the Female Body: Inspirational Icons* (2001), edited with Fan Hong. Also with Fan Hong, he has published *Soccer, Women, Sexual Liberation: Kicking Off a New Era* in celebration of the FIFA Women's World Cup in Beijing in 2003, dealing with the rise of women's association football largely as an outcome of middle-class feminist pressure for equality in sport.

In the early 1990s Mangan was certainly among the first, if not the first, to *re-emphasize* the powerful influence of the middle classes, bringing the middle classes back into focus in the history of modern sport in society, and stressing their key role. Elsewhere I have argued strongly for the extension of Mangan's concern for scholastic balance in class coverage, a concern he revealed early, preceding Peter Gay's recent concern over the neglect of the middle classes by a decade.[22] Mangan has explored the important question of middle-class motives and their intended and unintended consequences. His exploration of middle-class involvement in sport and society has continued to provide fresh and original perspectives. Recent revisionist volumes, for example, include *Reformers, Sport, Modernizers: Middle Class Revolutionaries* (2002) and *A Sport-Loving Society: Middle-Class Victorians and Edwardians at Play* (2003).

Mangan's re-emphasis on the middle classes has helped to balance the predominantly working-class research interests of many modern sports historians. A keen contributor to this latter approach was Richard Holt, whose neatly woven synthesis drew on new secondary sources in sports history about the working classes. His subsequent collection, *Sport and the Working Class in Modern Britain* had the expressed intention of 'making "submerged" identities and cultural traditions more visible', but its focus obscured rather than revealed hidden middle-class cultural traditions.[23] It was this dominant emphasis on working-class sporting culture that prompted John Lowerson's weary comment that 'with rare exceptions the major British attention has remained glued to working-class experience' and stimulated his own praiseworthy attempts to rescue the middle classes from some decades of neglect.[24] He has not been sparing, incidentally, in his praise of Mangan's middle class studies, remarking that Mangan's work on sport as a middle-class preparation for life – the athleticism, as Lowerson states, so 'brilliantly described' by him[25] – has covered the ground so well 'that any other historian now runs the serious risk of merely rehashing his ideas'.[26] In his later studies of the middle classes Mangan, too, took up the challenge to write them back into the history of sport. In his piece entitled 'Muscular, Militaristic and Manly: The British Middle Class Hero as Moral Messenger', he stated bluntly:

> The middle classes and the middle-class mythical heroes are firmly out of fashion. It is salutary, therefore, that they have a recorder. It ensures historical balance, rescues from conscious neglect a section of society which contributed hugely to national and world sport as a political, cultural and social entity, and arguably it avoids justifiable accusations of contemporary 'inverted snobbery'! In a period in which it is modish to embrace anti-elitism and eschew

elitism it is important in the interests of historical completeness that the middle-class athletic hero is not written out of cultural history.[27]

From the late 1980s, with the advent of the 'linguistic turn', class temporarily fell out of favour, and became viewed more as a 'construct of discourse', a way of organizing historical narratives. Writers such as Patrick Joyce moved away from class to focus more on the collective identities through which 'the people' represented themselves and the social order, a 'family of populisms' from workplace to neighbourhood, from town to region, or from religion to age and gender, and the conflicting or shared values these entailed. For Joyce, leisure, and therefore by implication sport (which regrettably he largely ignored), was a major vehicle in producing such populist cultural discourses.[28] British sports history picked up such themes directly in the innovatory work of Hill.[29] In Hill's work, however, it was the identity and outlook of the working classes that were the main focus. The middle classes were seen literally and metaphorically as mere spectators.

The late 1990s saw the impact of the 'linguistic turn' fade and the rise of a renewed and broader-based interest in the middle classes among the wider community of social historians. A conference, 'Aspects of the History of the British Middle Classes since 1750', held at Manchester Metropolitan University in 1996, contained detailed studies of aspects of Victorian middle-class life by (among others) Wahrman, Kidd and Nicholls, Tosh and Gunn.[30] Sport, however, figured surprisingly little, and it is certainly timely to re-evaluate the role of the English middle classes in bourgeois sporting culture, and re-stress their role in the evolution of modern sport. Some time ago I argued that right from the second half of the nineteenth century onward 'English middle-class sport increasingly functioned as a powerful cultural bond, moral metaphor and political symbol. It had a major influence on recreational culture, career access and the formation of class cultures and relationships.'[31] Its power, vitality, influence and status were immense both in Britain and abroad. It is to Mangan's credit that he has never stopped illustrating this. Sport articulated and expressed different forms of class relationship in different contexts, and different sports had very different class structures, and there is still much we do not know, and which needs to be teased out, in terms of middle-class involvement and cross-class links.

How exactly did sport affect the relationships within and between classes, in the countryside, towns and cities, and in different regions of Britain? In my own recent study of flat racing, for example, I was keen to set the sport firmly in the lives of all classes, and in relation to leisure cultures that cut across and existed within classes; such approaches may well apply to other sports.[32] All classes need consideration, although the upper classes are still inexcusably neglected in British sports historiography. Such approaches constitute a salutary search for *balance*, a way of encouraging a deeper and broader level of analysis and understanding of the evolution, assimilation, adaptation of and resistance to sport in culture.

Mangan, incidentally, is acutely concerned with balance in a global context. This is especially noticeable in his recent writing on imperialism and sport with his request for a much-needed 'triadic' approach to, for example, sport in modern Asia, involving Asia, the West and Asian and Western commentators. Perhaps one of his most valuable recent contributions to the evolution of the study of modern sport is his request for the voices of the former 'colonized' to be heard and their perspectives brought, through the English language, to Western readers. He practises what he preaches. Forthcoming collections such as *Sport in Asian Society: Past and Present* (with Fan Hong) and *Sport in South Asia Society: Past and Present* (with Boria Majumdar) certainly prove the point. Interestingly, Mangan has in passing called Cannadine gently to account for his strong emphasis on class as the defining element in imperialism and for not making more of colonial complexity – in this regard, in his recent study of the passionate imperial middle-class educationalist Alexander Garden Fraser, who worked idealistically for a Christian empire without class, religions or racial prejudices, castigated various obscenities of imperial capitalism and argued for a sensitive understanding of indigenous peoples, languages and cultures.[33]

The development and growth of (most particularly) the English middle classes between 1841 and 1901 was almost without parallel in the world, and established them as a highly significant and stable sector within British society. Their increased leisure time, their status in society, their income levels and work experience and their habit of late marriage all acted together to make their circumstances especially conducive to participation in sport. Other factors, including better health and nutrition, availability of land, or industrial technology were also important in sport's development, while advances in mass communication and transport had a more subsidiary part to play.[34] Middle-class individuals and institutions possessed a substantial measure of cultural authority. They had the power to shape, diversify and promulgate prevailing sporting tastes. Sports from hunting, shooting, yachting and horse-racing to tennis, golf, archery and croquet made their wealth and authority visible to their peers and to wider society.

The Victorian public schools, in all their variety, played a vital role as educational institutions in such developments. They developed the cult of athleticism, of course, which was soon extended into the grammar schools and on, in a modified form of middle-class manliness, into the elementary schools, areas of research to which Mangan has also contributed.[35] The public schools lay at the heart of Britain's imperial mission. They were the source of much later global sport, and in their late Victorian manifestations helped foster the codes of militaristic manliness, fair play and team spirit. There is still much of their imperial contribution to uncover. The forthcoming *Imperial Innovators: Soccer Schoolmasters Across the Globe* by Mangan (with Colm Hickey) no doubt will peel back a layer or two more.

In terms of their discussion of the adult sporting world, with a few honourable exceptions, sports historians have over-used the term 'middle class' rather than 'middle classes'. Their language has been over-broad and over-inclusive. As Cannadine has recently stressed in his revisionist attempt to rehabilitate 'class' as a legitimate subject of historical enquiry, 'there was no such thing as *the* late Victorian and Edwardian middle class: it was far too protean, varied and amorphous for that'.[36] It was divided in a whole variety of ways: horizontal divisions of income, property, status, social leadership or education competed with vertical divisions such as religious/denominational allegiance, political affiliation and splits between manufacturing, commercial and professional groups. There were also the more complex geographical divisions between north and south and between the middle classes in competing regions or cities such as Liverpool and Manchester. So what held this diversity of interests and opinions together, allowed social action to be taken and middle-class sporting culture to emerge? In the field of wider social history, Morris has argued that in the early Victorian period a key role was played by the wide, varied and complex network of voluntary societies. The literary and philosophical societies and choral societies were able to accommodate or transcend the competing interests of sect, party or income in a more neutral context and foster select sociability and cultural improvement.[37] When the first major sports boom occurred, the new sports associations had already-established institutions upon whom to model themselves, allowing members both to improve their play and enjoy sociability. Many middle-class sporting clubs, societies and organizations soon found in the ideologies of amateurism and the games ethic a useful way of encouraging sociability, minimizing competition and ensuring exclusivity within their ranks, a point also emphasized strongly by McKibbin in his study of the first half of the twentieth century.[38]

The amateur ethos survived in much British sport for around a hundred years, ultimately damaging Britain's sporting competitiveness and standing, and so it is unsurprising that many surveys of British sport have provided chapters on the topic.[39] At times the language of such discussion can confuse the unwary, with its talk of 'elites', 'gentlemen' or 'governing bodies'. Such language can unintentionally render the middle classes invisible; by making them appear to be absent from the discussion we can underestimate their role. Holt, for example, talks of the 'gentleman amateur' in Victorian Britain, although his subsequent discussion makes clear that the supposed 'gentleman' was from the middle as well as the upper classes.[40] Wigglesworth is more open to criticism in his use of language. His discussion of amateurism portrays British society as divided between 'gentlemen' and 'working' men and women. In reality, the title of 'gentleman' was commonly claimed, used and abused. It was most often self-ascribed. It could be employed in a variety of ways by different groups in society. As a result any use of the term needs to be clearly contextualized, which Wigglesworth fails to do.[41] The role of the middle classes was often critical in sustaining amateur attitudes and much more clarity is needed than hereto in drawing out their role, the ways in which they were active and the means they employed.

The English middle classes were pre-eminent among early international innovators of sport, and thus played *the* key role in the establishment and early development of modern sport – sports that are leading elements in modern global culture. The latter too is a field to which Mangan has made telling contributions. He has extended his studies of the diffusion of the games ethic beyond England and across the globe, providing a range of fascinating examples which include studies of the ways in which Scottish pioneer educationists became exponents of a British identity for the Scots middle classes, or the extent to which the early evolution of modern sport in Latin America was a mainly English middle-class inspiration.[42] Because of Mangan we now know more about how sport and the sports field are intimately linked to the complex politics of colonialism, imperialism, decolonialism and nationalism, and the role which middle-class institutions played in this. Mangan's role in all this is discussed more fully elsewhere in this volume.

As stated earlier, not all sports historians have shown a liking for an exploration of working-class culture, still less of a liking for middle-class sporting ideologies and life, but interest in professional sport and sportsmen has not been all-encompassing. Halladay, for example, in his history of the minority sport of amateur rowing and its relation to the tradition of artisan rowing, discussed the upper-middle class and its efforts to involve itself in the issues of amateurism as a means of moral assertion and moral indoctrination. This was part of a strong thrust towards social engineering on the one hand and social distancing on the other.[43] Lowerson, like Mangan, has been a leading figure in opening up the middle classes to more careful historical investigation. His personal interests in such topics as golf, bowls and fishing helped in the production of what has been thus far the most detailed study of sport and the English middle classes, published in 1993.[44] This marked by far the most detailed account of the active recreations of the adult middle classes in the still relatively raw and ever-increasingly urban and industrial society of Victorian and Edwardian England. It was scholarly, gracefully written, well researched and replete with much regional material which provided an impressive breadth of coverage, including even minority middle-class sports such as badminton, climbing or croquet neglected by most historians. Scholars have recently given more attention to middle-class sports, from skating to archery. Building on the foundations laid by Mangan, Lowerson and others, a 'thought-provoking' and 'timely understanding' of middle-class involvement in the expanding sports of the Victorian and Edwardian era, has increasingly been sought.[45]

What else is left to explore of middle-class sporting life? The agenda is still, frankly, substantial. The post-educational field is the area that has suffered most neglect and needs most detailed scrutiny. Many of the sports popular with the adult middle classes were little practised at either school or university, although even here the coverage of athleticism's spread is still somewhat patchy in terms of London, the provincial towns and the rural areas.

Firstly, the role of London, the metropolitan centre, in terms of shaping middle-class sporting experience has yet to be fully brought out. We need a far fuller history of London sport. The expansion of sport was initially a metropolitan middle-class phenomenon, with its roots partly in the suburbs, which still need much more careful coverage as major middle-class communities, just as were the public schools. But in rugby, football and even in sports such as rowing, the revolt of the provinces against the domination of London and its suburbs was to profoundly change the nature of the sports themselves. Many of the northern middle classes most closely connected with the promotion of professional team sports had little direct contact with the ideology of athleticism, and relatively little sympathy with the behavioural values of amateurism. Why was the southern view so differently balanced? One possible explanation might well be the far higher proportion of public-school old boys who settled in and around London; but we need to dig much deeper to find answers.

Second, research has focused substantially on middle-class institutional cultural and sporting structures and ideologies. We need to move from these to explore in more detail what sport actually meant to the middle classes themselves, both in terms of what they gained socially from their membership and what it meant affectively. The deeper analysis of the enjoyable experience of such middle-class sporting institutions still needs more consideration. What recent research has begun to make ever clearer is that the simplistic social divisions between 'respectables', 'roughs' and 'hedonists' were far more fluid than has been supposed, and cannot be used in assigning stereotypical social class or leisure culture identities. Individuals moved in and out of them, depending on contexts.[46]

Conventional wisdom about the supposed triumph of Victorian middle-class respectability needs to be reassessed. The reality was far more complex, fluid and inchoate than has been commonly supposed. 'Respectability' often lay as much in the status of those taking part as in the activity itself. The participation of the 'right' people could confer respectability; that of the wrong people could deny it. Equally many activities could be privately enjoyed that might have been seen in different ways if the light of adverse publicity had illuminated them. Most middle-class Victorians were happy to adopt the Nelsonian perspective of the blind eye to ensure their self-preservation when it came to such pleasures, and scandal and corruption may well have been more common than hitherto realized. Members of cycling, football, cricket, rugby and even prestigious harrier clubs all at times unashamedly enjoyed the attraction of more 'sinful' pleasures in private.[47] Walton has recently perceived the 'beginning of a much wider reinterpretation of nineteenth-century British society'. He sees the viability of the synthesis now coming under 'direct challenge', in large part through recent work on sport and leisure.[48] Such reinterpretations challenge aspects of the 'rise of respectable society', the 'civilizing process' and orthodox accounts of 'the importance of Evangelical religion, the acceptance of formal policing, and above all the internalization of habits of deferred gratification, thrift, self-control, gravity, continence and economic rationality'. As Lowerson once remarked, 'the middle classes have often demonstrated remarkable competence at covering their tracks'.[49]

Third, although there has been a limited amount of work already done on the importance of mass-circulation newspapers and specialist sports publications, little work has yet been carried out on the background of the leading sports journalists of the nineteenth century. In horse-racing, the field where I have most background knowledge, the classical references in the reports, the style of writing and the biographies of several leading journalists in the field all suggest that a majority had middle-class backgrounds, with a substantial number of these having been to public school.[50]

Fourth, the lower stratum of the middle class, those lower status groups comprising white-collar/grey collar occupations such as clerks, small wholesalers and retailers/shopkeepers, who had no chance of a public-school education, has been neglected in a major way. Many had sufficient education to have played a key role as secretaries, chairmen or treasurers of sports societies. At the local level, the availability of census material and the lists of officials, with addresses published in newspapers and directories, should allow nominal record linkage to establish the extent of their involvement.[51]

Fifth, most sports historians have fought shy of exploring the complex inter-relationships between religion, sport and the middle classes.[52] In some sections of the sporting press in the nineteenth century the church was seen as dull, boring and irrelevant, and this process of apostasy became stronger in the twentieth century. Sports historians of the nineteenth century have overemphasized the progress of the secular movement. Sometimes they have failed to appreciate the positive contributions of the religious groups, preferring to stress their role as radical reformers, espousers of 'muscular Christianity' and attackers of cruel sports, or their role as social controllers through Sabbatarian attitudes. Yet the influence of the churches was important. It is clear that Anglican leaders soon resigned themselves to the sports boom, and accepted it as recreation for work. The nonconformists, first trying to check its spread, soon tried to control it by creating cricket, football and other sports clubs. Their role in the initial creation of so many clubs has been recognized, but not linked to the middle classes. Many young clergymen played games and encouraged others to do so. The public schools too need more work in relation to sport and religion.

Mangan, of course, has explored issues of muscular Christianity, Roman Catholic apostasy and Christian gentility in some detail in relation to the public schools. He also explored the motivations of various head teachers, for whom religion often had a role to play, not least since most heads were also clergymen, and he has demonstrated the differences between the attitudes to athleticism in Catholic Stonyhurst and the other schools in his study. But what of Ampleforth or Downside? What too of dissenting schools? There was a parallel system of boarding schools which included the Congregationalists' Mill Hill (1808), the Methodists' Kingswood (1748) and The Leys, Cambridge (1875) and the Society of Friends' schools such as Ackworth (1771) which would all repay study. The extent to which nonconformity took on the values of athleticism would certainly be illuminating. There is a real need to integrate the existing disparate material and produce a fuller picture of the relationship between sport, religion and class. Over and over again, Mangan, of course, to his credit, has urged research on the public schools to continue. The last word has emphatically not been said.

Sixth, and finally, and following on from the last point, as yet no one has examined the middle-class involvement in sport in the twentieth century in any detail. There is nothing to parallel Mangan's work on the Victorian and Edwardian schools and university sporting world. The world of twentieth-century middle-class sport is now beginning to be explored, although still in far less detail than its importance has deserved.[53]

The social theorist W.G. Runciman has recently presented powerful and fairly convincing arguments that fundamental societal-level changes in social, economic and political practice and resultant shifting patterns of class were a result of the First and not the Second World War.[54] McKibbin argues, in his *Classes and Cultures: England, 1918–1951*, that inter-war Britain was characterized by a major divide between manual and non-manual workers and that leisure, lifestyle and employment created subcultures which he calls 'working-class culture' and 'middle-class culture'. In terms of sport, however, we need further work to support or challenge this view. My own view is that some at least among the middle classes were always attracted, through a variety of reasons, to more supposedly 'working-class' sports, including those sports associated with drink and gambling. To some, perhaps, this was due to their earlier working-class origins, to others the attractions of 'slumming', sheer pleasure in the sport or the cultural hedonism of a homo-social subgroup. By the inter-war period, while social distinctions were still expressed in class terms, social roles were much more fluid and dependent on social context. A polarized dichotomous view of class might be embraced at work but not in wider social relationships. There might be strong consciousness of status divisions within a middle-class group, yet the group might present a solid face to the world. The spatial aspects of class, expressed in the more middle-class ethos of the suburbs, and the more working-class community feel of terraced city streets or newly-built council estates, clearly had an effect. But there were manual labourers in the suburbs, and clerks in city streets, each perhaps embracing or standing against locally dominant cultural sporting practices.

For some, too, among the middle classes the weekend football match, the filling in of the pools coupon or a bet on the Grand National could be danger zones to be avoided. For others, however, they offered major sources of pleasure. It has been claimed that 'the middle classes rarely betted on sport'.[55] This was a tacit acceptance of a dominant and carefully constructed middle-class myth. For some among the middle classes, betting was far too resilient a pleasure to be avoided, although since much of their betting was on credit, or through the purchase of sweeps, it has until recently remained hidden. My forthcoming work on horse racing and British culture between 1919 and 1939 will examine in some detail middle-class involvement in the excitements and risks of betting, as part of a broader exploration of the place of racing in British society.[56]

The fit between cultural practice and occupation was by this period not always a close one. Sport has never been enjoyed by all, and each sport possessed its own intrinsic as well as its own cultural appeal, while the cult of amateurism was already under significant public attack in some quarters. To remedy some of the continuing deficiencies in our understanding we need to pay more careful attention to its place in class and culture than hitherto, and most especially the key cultural roles played by the middle classes.

In conclusion, 2003 will see 20 years of *BJSH/IJHS* under one founding editor – no mean achievement. In 1984, when the forerunner of the *IJHS*, *The British Journal of Sports History*, was founded, it had the avowed intent to provide a forum for the 'discussion of new approaches, ideas and information' about sport, recreation and leisure. It also wished to draw on 'contributions from allied disciplines'. Mangan's work, bringing to bear as it does insights drawn from history, anthropology, sociology and cultural studies, has provided a sophisticated, subtle and highly suggestive set of responses to that request. Arguably, he above all, has helped to foreground the Victorian middle classes and their central role in the creation and spread of modern sports, providing revisionist perspectives from which many have gained new insights and undoubtedly others will gain further insights in the future.

NOTES

1. Jeff Hill, 'British Sports History: A Post-Modern Future', *Journal of Sport History*, 23,1 (1996), 5–6, 11.
2. R.W. Malcolmson, *Popular Recreations in English Society, 1700–1850* (Cambridge: Cambridge University Press, 1973).
3. Peter Bailey, *Leisure and Class in Victorian England: Rational Recreation and the Contest for Control* (London: Methuen, 1987).
4. See Brian Simon and Ian Bradley (eds), *The Victorian Public School* (Dublin: Gill Macmillan, 1975).
5. J.A. Mangan, *Physical Education and Sport: Sociological and Cultural Perspectives* (Oxford: Oxford University Press, 1973).
6. Recently reissued with a new introduction and introductory sections by Sheldon Rothblatt and Jeffrey Richards as J.A. Mangan, *Athleticism in the Victorian and Edwardian Public School: The Emergence and Consolidation of an Educational Ideology* (London and Portland, OR: Frank Cass, 2000).
7. Mike Huggins, 'Review Essay: Athleticism in the Victorian and Edwardian Public School', *The International Journal of the History of Sport*, 18, 4 (2001), 149–55.
8. See Mangan, *Athleticism*, pp.2–4, for a succinct description of the various kinds of nineteenth-century public schools.
9. John Lowerson, *Sport and the English Middle Classes, 1870–1914* (Manchester: Manchester University Press, 1993), p.72.
10. E. Royle, *Modern Britain: A Social History 1750–1997* (London: Arnold, 1997) pp.365–6.
11. Jeremy Paxman, *The English: The Portrait of a People* (London: Penguin, 1999), p.196.
12. See Mike Huggins, 'Walking in the Footsteps of a Pioneer: Peter McIntosh – Trailblazer in the History of Sport', *The International Journal of the History of Sport*, 18, 2 (June 2001), 136–47.

13. See in particular, Sheldon Rothblatt, *The Revolution of the Dons: Cambridge and Society in Victorian England* (Cambridge: Cambridge University Press, 1968); Christopher Hibbert, *No Ordinary Place: Radley College and the Public School System 1847–1997* (London: John Murray, 1997).

14. Clive Dewey, 'Socratic Teachers Part 1– the Opposition to the Games Cult of Athletics at Eton, 1870–1914', *The International Journal of the History of Sport*, 12, 2 (1995).

15. Neil Tranter, *Sport, Economy and Society in Britain 1750–1914* (Cambridge: Cambridge University Press, 1998), pp.44–6.

16. My forthcoming book *Sport and the Victorians* (London: Hambledon Press, 2004) will discuss this in more detail.

17. See J.A. Mangan, 'Games Field and Battlefield: A Romantic Alliance in Verse and the Creation of Militaristic Masculinity', in John Nauright and Timothy J.L. Chandler (eds), *Making Men: Rugby and Masculine Identity* (London and Portland, OR: Frank Cass, 1996), pp. 140–57.

18. J.A. Mangan, 'Grammar Schools and the Games Ethic in the Victorian and Edwardian Eras', *Albion*, 15, 5 (1983).

19. J.A. Mangan, 'Oars and the Man: Pleasure and Purpose in Victorian and Edwardian Cambridge', *History of Higher Education Annual 1984*, 52–77; J.A. Mangan, 'Lamentable Barbarians and Pitiful Sheep: The Rhetoric of Protest and Pleasure in Late Victorian and Edwardian Oxbridge', in Tom Winnifrith and Cyril Barrett (eds), *Leisure in Art and Literature* (Basingstoke: Macmillan, 1992); J.A. Mangan and Callum McKenzie, 'The Other Side of the Coin: Masculinity, Victorian Field Sports and English Elite Education', *European Sports History Review*, 2 (1999), 59–82.

20. Lowerson, *Sport and the English Middle Classes*, pp.75–6.

21. David Rubenstein, *Before the Suffragettes: Women's Emancipation in the 1890s* (Brighton: Harvester Press, 1986); J.A. Mangan and R.J. Park (eds), *From 'Fair Sex' to Feminism: Sport and the Socialization of Women in the Industrial and Post-Industrial Eras* (London: Frank Cass, 1987).

22. See J.A. Mangan and James Walvin (eds), *Manliness and Morality: Middle-Class Masculinity in Britain and America, 1800–1940* (Manchester: Manchester University Press, 1987); Peter Gay, *Schnitzler's Century: The Making of Middle-Class Culture 1815–1914* (London: Allen Lane, 2001).

23. Richard Holt, *Sport and the British* (Oxford: Oxford University Press, 1989); Richard Holt (ed.), *Sport and the Working Class in Modern Britain* (Manchester: Manchester University Press, 1990), p.3.

24. John Lowerson, 'Opiate of the People and Stimulant for the Historian? Some Issues in Sports History', in W. Lamont (ed.), *Historical Controversies and Historians* (London: UCL Press, 1998), p.209.

25. See Lowerson, *Sport and the English Middle Classes*, p.3.

26. Ibid., p.19.

27. In Richard Holt, J.A. Mangan and P. Lanfranchi (eds), *European Heroes: Myth, Identity, Sport* (London and Portland, OR: Frank Cass, 1996), p.44.

28. Patrick Joyce, *Visions of the People: Industrial England and the Question of Class* (Cambridge: Cambridge University Press, 1991) and *Democratic Subjects: The Self and the Social in Nineteenth Century England* (Cambridge: Cambridge University Press, 1994).

29. See, for example, Jeff Hill and Jack Williams (eds), *Sport and Identity in the North of England* (Keele: Keele University Press, 1996).

30. Drew Wahrman, *Imagining the Middle Class: The Political Representation of Class in Britain c.1780–1840* (Cambridge: Cambridge University Press, 1995); A.J. Kidd and D. Nicholls (eds), *The Making of the British Middle Class?: Studies of Regional and Cultural Diversity since the Eighteenth Century* (Stroud: Sutton Press, 1998); A.J. Kidd and D. Nicholls (eds), *Gender, Civic Culture and Consumerism: Middle-Class Identity in Britain 1800–1940* (Manchester: Manchester University Press, 1999); Simon Gunn, *The Public Culture of the Victorian Middle Class: Ritual and Authority and the English Industrial City* (Manchester: Manchester University Press, 2000).

31. Mike Huggins, 'Second-Class Citizens? English Middle-Class Culture and Sport 1850–1910:

A Reconsideration', *The International Journal of the History of Sport*, 17,1 (2000), 1.

32. Mike Huggins, *Flat Racing and British Society 1790-1914* (London and Portland, OR: Frank Cass, 2000).

33. See J.A. Mangan, 'Imperial Origins: Christian Manliness, Moral Imperatives and Pre-Sri Lankan Playing Fields – Beginnings' in J.A. Mangan and Fan Hong (eds.), *Sport in Asian Society: Past and Present* (London and Portland, OR: Frank Cass, 2003).

34. For a critique of earlier views of the importance of the railways in sport's development, see Mike Huggins and John Tolson, 'The Railways and Sport in Victorian Britain: A Critical Reassessment', *Journal of Transport History*, 22, 2 (2001), 99–115.

35. J.A. Mangan and Colm Hickey, 'Athleticism in the Service of the Proletariat: Preparation for the Elementary School and the Extension of Middle-Class Manliness', in J.A. Mangan, *Sport, Europe, Gender: Making European Masculinities* (London and Portland, OR: Frank Cass, 2000).

36. David Cannadine, *Class in Britain* (New Haven, CT: Yale University Press, 1998), p.121.

37. R.J. Morris, *Class. Sect and Party: The Making of the British Middle Class: Leeds 1820–1850* (Manchester: Manchester University Press, 1990).

38. Ross McKibbin, *Classes and Cultures*: England, 1918–1951 (Oxford: Oxford University Press, 1998), pp.377ff.

39. See Richard Holt and Tony Mason, *Sport in Britain 1945–2000* (Oxford: Blackwell, 2000); Neil Wigglesworth, *The Evolution of British Sport* (London and Portland, OR: Frank Cass, 1996); Richard Holt, *Sport and the British: A Modern History* (Oxford: Clarendon Press, 1989).

40. Holt, *Sport and the British*, p.98.

41. Wigglesworth, *Evolution of British Sport*, pp. 84–107.

42. J.A. Mangan, 'Braveheart Betrayed? Cultural Cloning for Imperial Careers', *Immigrants and Minorities*, 17,1 (1998), 189–208.

43. Eric Halladay, *Rowing in England: A Social History* (Manchester: Manchester University Press, 1990).

44. Lowerson, *Sport and the English Middle Classes*.

45. J.A. Mangan, 'Introduction to the New Edition', *Athleticism in the Victorian and Edwardian Public School* (London and Portland, OR: Frank Cass, 2000) p.xlix; Mike Huggins, 'Second Class Citizens? English Middle Class Culture and Sport 1850–1914: A Reconsideration', *The International Journal of the History of Sport*, 17,1 (2000).

46. Mike Huggins, 'More Sinful Pleasures? Leisure, Respectability and the Male Middle Classes in Victorian England', *Journal of Social History*, 33, 3 (2000), 585–600.

47. See Mike Huggins and J.A. Mangan (eds), *Disreputable Recreations: Less-Virtuous Victorians at Play* (London and Portland, OR: Frank Cass, 2003).

48. John K. Walton, review of Huggins, *Flat Racing and British Society*, *Journal of Social History*, 34,2 (2001), 488.

49. John Lowerson, 'Sporting Metaphors and New Marathons: The Vitality of the Middle-Class Legacy', *The International Journal of the History of Sport*, 17,4 (2000), 113.

50. Tony Mason, *Association Football and English Society 1863–1915* (Brighton: Harvester Press, 1980), pp.189, 195.

51. Paul Blackledge, 'Rationalist Capitalist Concerns: William Cail and the Great Rugby Split of 1895', *The International Journal of the History of Sport*, 18,2 (2001), 35–53.

52. Some exploration of the links is illustrated in J. Hoffman, *Sport and Religion* (Champagne, IL: Human Kinetics, 1992).

53. Jack Williams, *Cricket and England: A Cultural and Social History of the Inter-war Years* (London and Portland, OR: Frank Cass, 1999).

54. W.G. Runciman, *A Treatise on Social Theory*, Vol.III: *Applied Social Theory* (Cambridge: Cambridge University Press, 1997).

55. McKibbin, *Classes and Cultures*, p.371.

56. Mike Huggins, *Horseracing and the British 1919–1939* (Manchester: Manchester University Press, 2003).

5

Pathfinding and Pathmaking:
J.A. Mangan and Imperialism,
Education and Socialization

COLM FINTAN HICKEY

INTRODUCTION

Professor James (Tony) Mangan has written prodigiously and prolifically on a range of issues related to athleticism, masculinity and imperialism. He has published as author, co-author, editor and co-editor at least 30 publications and innumerable articles – many dealing implicitly or explicitly with these issues.[1] His work is widely admired in Britain, Europe and globally. Undoubtedly his most famous work, *Athleticism in the Victorian and Edwardian Public School: The Emergence and Consolidation of an Educational Ideology*, first published by Cambridge University Press in 1981, brought fresh perspectives to the history of the public school. In his introduction to the Frank Cass Edition in 2000, Jeffrey Richards commented that the book was: 'awesomely scholarly and meticulously documented'.[2] In his foreword to the same volume, Sheldon Rothblatt of the University of California at Berkeley wrote that 'Mangan has . . . become one of the leading – perhaps the leading – scholar, certainly a leader of scholars, in developing, reformulating and extending the comparative dimensions of sports in relation to society and culture in a highly international perspective'.[3] As part of this international perspective, a major Mangan contribution to cultural history has been in the field of imperialism. His second book, *The Games Ethic and Imperialism: Aspects of the Diffusion of an Ideal*, arguably is even more influential internationally than *Athleticism*. In his Introduction to the 1986 Viking Penguin edition, he wrote:

> As the story in its full complexity cannot be told here, it is intended that further instalments will appear in due course, in forthcoming

studies of the ethic. . . . Even then, of course, completeness will not
have been achieved. And it is to be hoped that, in time, others will
repair omissions, reveal fresh facets, add subtlety when required,
and so augment my early and exploratory efforts. Consideration of
this influential ideology is long overdue. The outcome of Waterloo
would certainly have been the same without the existence of the
Eton wall-game: the nature of the Empire would scarcely have
been the same without the public school games ethic.[4]

Unquestionably this is the case.

True to his word, there have been additional instalments from his pen,
dealing with 'direct' cultural imperialism in, for example, Ceylon (Sri
Lanka) in his recently (edited with Fan Hong) published *Sport in Asian
Society: Past and Present* (2001) and in Japan (with Ikuo Abe) in the same
volume.

In addition, there is a chapter on the influence of English athleticism
in Argentina ('the unclaimed colony') in his co-edited (with Lamartine
DaCosta) *Sport in Latin American Society: Past and Present* (2001). And,
of course, there were his collections on empire and sport entitled
*Pleasure, Profit and Proselytism: British Culture and Sport at Home and
Abroad* (1988); *Sport in Africa: Essays in Social History* (with William J.
Baker); and *The Cultural Bond: Sport, Empire, Society* (1992). All three
collections contain seminal contributions by the editor.

What is not always adequately appreciated is that his writing on
imperialism has gone well beyond consideration of sport, morality and
gender in imperial contexts. He has edited and written authoritatively in
collections on the socialization of the dominant and dominated and
colonialism. There is *'Benefits Bestowed'? Education and British
Imperialism* (1988); *Making Imperial Mentalities: Socialization and
British Imperialism* (1990); and *The Imperial Curriculum: Racial Images
and Education in the British Colonial Experience* (1993).

This article has three parts: the first is an analysis of Mangan's
writings on imperialism, the second is a case study of an attempt to
propagate imperialism in the Egyptian educational system, which
illustrates his analytical influence, and the third is a brief assessment of
the impact of Mangan's work and his contributions to new and hitherto
unexplored seams in the mine of the history of imperialism, education
and socialization.

MANGAN ON IMPERIALISM

In the last 20 years Mangan has reshaped both our thinking and our understanding of imperialism. In the first instance he has helped provide us with useful caveats concerning this often unexplained term, illustrating his own relentless search for judicious judgements. As he has written, in some contexts, 'whether imperialism was a form of widespread benevolence or an unmitigated evil is beside the point'.[5] He has also remarked that imperialism ' is a word to be used with extreme caution. It is as likely to confuse as to clarify, lacks an agreed meaning and is open to many interpretations.' While he favours the definition provided by George Nadel and Perry Curtis for its sharp clarity – 'the extension of sovereignty or control, whether direct or indirect, political or economic, by one government, nation or society over another together with the ideas justifying or opposing this process'[6] – he is quick to point out that the definition has severe limitations, ignoring, for instance, imperialism as a 'cultural umbilical cord'. However, he believes that 'This fact should not necessarily be a source of despair, irritation or criticism. Imperialism was an extraordinarily complex phenomenon. Only by acknowledging the multiple meanings given to it, can its full role in British affairs – and education – be obtained.'[7]

One strength of his work is that he has greatly added to these multiple meanings, especially in his detailed considerations of sport as an imperial moral mechanism, a source of social control and an instrument of 'tribal' cohesion. Another strength is his emphasis on the importance of education as a form of cultural cloning in the imperial endeavour. Where imperialism has been considered, he has pointed out, there has been an almost complete omission of education, not only by imperial historians but by educational historians as well. Indeed, 'most general histories of British (and English) education can be read without any realization that Britain was an imperial power in the eighteenth, nineteenth and twentieth centuries.'[8] While there have been any number of individual studies of regions, institutions or individuals, 'little of this work has been integrated into imperial overviews'. Part of the problem, of course, as he shrewdly observes, is that 'historians of all persuasions have paid too little attention to socialization, as opposed to social change'.[9] Early in his own publications, therefore, he asserted that it was 'surely now time to turn to barer patches on the imperial canvas and begin to fill them in'.[10]

Mangan argues cogently that we need to build on the work of Harold Silver who, in *Education as History*, argued:

The history of education is in fact multiple histories because education is itself no simple and homogeneous concept or category, and because its history can be explored in relation to almost endless variables. Whether education is conceived as itself an identifiable cluster of experiences or as a more narrowly definable process related to a variety of other processes, it has no meaning when presented in isolated and discretely institutional terms.[11]

Silver's subtle argument finds much favour with Mangan. He believes that Silver's view

raises still further and more difficult questions about present and past limitations of perspective about disciplinary and sub-disciplinary boundaries (and sensible and amiable transgression) and about adequate methodologies: 'a pre-requisite of cross-cultural history across frontiers . . . has to be sustained dialogue among (all types of) historians, not only about the cross-cultural meaning and possibilities, but also about cross-disciplinary experience.'[12]

Silver offered a new vision for the interpretation of educational history: firstly, accountability, examining different perceptions of educational and political relationships; secondly, the history of adolescence; thirdly, reform, at national and community level; and lastly, ideological considerations. Mangan is quick to support this vision and as quick to provide empirical evidence as support. In this setting he finds much to agree with in the comments of Joan Simon, who believes that 'educational processes lie at the heart of things'.[13] She adds, clearly to his nod of approval, that 'it might be regarded as the core of history since social achievements are stored in an external, esoteric form and must be mastered by each generation'.[14]

For Mangan the views of Silver and Simon carry much weight. He believes that if Simon is correct, 'then education with its close association to politics, economics, religion and social structure, lends itself especially well to a new and ambitious commonality of intellectual effort'.[15] It is Mangan's contribution to this new commonality of intellectual effort that I will now briefly explore further.

In the companion volume to *'Benefits Bestowed'?*, *Making Imperial Mentalities: Socialization and British Imperialism*, Mangan discussed the impact of political socialization on education. It can be viewed in both narrow and broad focus: the former as 'the deliberate inculcation of political knowledge, values and practices by agents and agencies formally charged with this responsibility'[16] and the latter as 'not only political but also apparently non-political learning, formal and informal, calculated and uncalculated, which effects the learning of politically relevant individual and group behaviour'.[17] Political socialization is concerned with acceptance of, and compliance with, the dominant ideology and the dominant group acts as a significant agent of socialization and 'as an innovatory, then as a stabilizing and finally as a conserving influence.'[18] Writing of political socialization, Mangan suggests that

> In any consideration of this phenomenon concepts such as indoctrination, induction, inculcation, assimilation, adaptation and adjustment are significant terms. And these terms in turn stimulate important questions: among them, what is the relationship between early indoctrination and adult orientation, what are the various formal and informal mechanisms adopted in attempts to ensure ideological conformity and compliance, and, most pertinently perhaps, how effective are these mechanisms in the reality of everyday life in situations of competing cultural demands and in contexts of superiority and inferiority?[19]

These are compelling questions which allow us to 're-engineer' our thinking and consider afresh what may have been previously unchallenged constructs of the British imperial story. By *closely* examining the actions, motives and beliefs of both the superior and subordinate groups we may be able to produce ever more compelling and satisfying accounts of historical change and development. A further Mangan observation is worthy of our close consideration: 'Youth, it has been observed, has the greater facility to adapt to severe cultural change. In consequence, strenuous efforts made by the dominant to socialize the young have been a feature of imperialism.'[20]

Mangan posits two elements of imperial socialization: the first, enculturation as the aggressive induction into the dominant culture and, second, acculturation as 'the process of acquiring more passively, through contact, elements of this culture'.[21] He insists that we must be aware of the fact that the socialization of the colonizer and the colonized was highly complex: 'There were a multiplicity of agents of contact, different phases of contact, degrees of contact, varying means of contact and various methods of contact.'[22] Accordingly, we must be cautious about making statements that are too general and therefore lack accuracy, and statements that are too abstract and have little contextual validity. These are important reminders. In short, Mangan is always aware that we need to be aware of the subtleties of imperialism and the multiplicity of ways in which it was interpreted by colonizer and colonized. At the same time he does not lose sight of the fact that imperialism had an imperial cultural constant. In *The Cultural Bond: Sport, Empire, Society*, he refers to the work of A.L. Kroeber and G. Kluckholn,[23] who have argued that culture has, at its core historically derived and selected ideas and their attached values and that cultural systems are both the products and determinants of social action. As Mangan himself puts it: 'In short, culture is essentially a set of potent and dynamic normative ideas, beliefs and actions.'[24]

In this regard, Mangan has argued seminally and persuasively that:

> It is time that it was more widely recognized that by the late nineteenth century sport lay close to the heart of Britain's imperial culture. It formed a distinct, persistent and significant cluster of cultural traits isolated in time and space, possessing a coherent structure and definite purpose. While it had many cultural functions, it had certainly become a means of propagating imperial sentiments. [25]

Study of these sentiments, as Patrick Bratlinger has claimed, has shown that any history must include ramifications in town, city, colony and dominion.[26] This Mangan has done extensively.

Sport in imperialism, Mangan adamantly insists, therefore, is an important element of cultural history. Furthermore, it should be viewed within a context of historical, anthropological and sociological concepts and constructs. This enables us to generate new hypotheses about the relationship between it and cultural ideas and processes.

I have mentioned earlier Mangan's equally strong insistence that sport was as much an intended source of social cohesion – a cultural bond – as it was a means of social control. This imperial bonding was effected by means of sports rituals, myths and symbols which were acted and re-enacted and served as powerful instruments of cohesion, loyalty and emulation. Sport was an influential manifestation of shared values. It was a blueprint 'for the organization of social and psychological processes much as generic systems provide such a template for the organization of organic processes'.[27] Thus for Mangan sport can be on occasion 'far more meaningful at home and abroad than literature, music, art or religion'.[28]

Sport, therefore, was a major component of Britain's imperial expression. Allied to education, indeed as a central element of the educative process, it certainly occupied an integral place in the schools of the elite. And recent research has demonstrated that it was not confined to the schools of the privileged. Both at home and abroad athleticism (in adapted form) and imperialism were essential features of the education of those who were educated in imperial elementary schools.[29]

Some of the best of Mangan's work has centred upon the work, roles and actions of a host of imperial proselytizers, men who with passion and purpose, clarity and conviction, forcefully and frequently espoused a view of an idiosyncratically British imperialism. At the heart of personal idiosyncratic imperial expression was the space and time given to games in formal and informal settings. Mangan's studies of Cecil Earle Tyndale Biscoe, Alexander Garden Fraser, John Guthrie Kerr and Hely Hutchinson Almond are substantial contributions to the biographies of imperial educationists – at home and abroad. *Inter alia*, they have stimulated others to explore the initiatives of others in parts of empire to which Mangan has as yet not turned his attention. One example – Egypt, discussed below – is a location in which in the discussion his influence is happily apparent, and in which there is an attempt briefly to assess the extent to which British 'imperial values' were adopted and adapted by the colonized themselves. Egypt is a particularly interesting country as it had a long tradition of interaction with a number of European nations before being administered by Britain from 1882.

IMPERIALISM AND EGYPT:
THE BOROUGH ROAD EXPERIMENT

For over 50 years Egypt had been run by the Khedive Muhammed Ali and his successors as little more than a vast private estate. Two-fifths of the country's cultivated land had been given over to the growing of cotton, the majority of which was exported to Britain. This economic expansion had been paid for through loans from Britain and France – so much so that in 1880 Egypt's debts were £100 million, while her annual exports were only £13 million. To alleviate the problem, Khedive Ismail had sold 44 per cent of his holding in the Suez Canal for £4 million to Britain in 1875. Nevertheless, the country was lurching into bankruptcy. In 1879, an international conference forced the new Khedive Tawfiq to accept Anglo-French control of his treasury, customs, post offices, telegraphs railways and ports. Predictably enough this measure provoked a nationalist backlash, headed by Urabi Pasha, who led a *coup d'état* in 1881.

Viewed from the perspectives of the time, as far as Britain was concerned, this was something that could not be tolerated. In July 1882, Gladstone's government authorized the bombardment and occupation of Alexandria under forces led by Admiral Sir Beauchamp Seymour. Furthermore, 31,000 troops led by General Wolseley defeated Urabi at Tel-el-Kebir and occupied Cairo. It was in this way that Egypt became a semi-imperial possession of Britain: not being a mandate, dominion or colony nevertheless, but a significant aspect of the imperial political diaspora. Lawrence James explains that:

> What had been created in Egypt was an imperial hybrid. It was neither a colony nor an official protectorate, and outwardly it remained an independent country ruled by a Khedive, whose overlord was, in purely legal terms, the Sultan of Turkey. In reality Egypt was, after 1882, a state where power rested in the hands of a higher civil service staffed by British officials, whose first priority was to bring the country to solvency.[30]

The annexation of Egypt was something that made the British Prime Minister, Gladstone, deeply uncomfortable. Two years earlier, the Liberals 'had campaigned against the amoral adventurism of the Tories and in favour of a pacific foreign policy based on international co-operation'.[31] Furthermore, the move sat very uncomfortably with Gladstone's position on issues such as Home Rule for Ireland. As Richard Shannon explains in *The Crisis of Imperialism*:

> For the next two and half years of his second ministry Gladstone regularly announced that Britain was in Egypt for the good of the Egyptians and as the executor of European will, and would withdraw, in the words of the famous Granville circular to the Great Powers of January 1885, 'as soon as the state of the country and the organisation of proper maintenance of Khedival authority

will admit to it'. But since the British presence was necessary to preserve the Khedival authority in the first place, the maintenance of that authority would depend on a continued British occupation. Gladstone and the Liberals never managed to evade that simple logic.[32]

This policy was to have significant ramifications for education. The man responsible for the administration of Egypt, from 1882 until his retirement in 1907, was Sir Evelyn Baring (later the Earl of Cromer).[33] His *idée maîtresse* was that there should not be a highly developed literary education available for the mass of the Egyptians. And while he wanted to see the expansion of elementary education, it was a functionalist rather than a liberal programme he advocated:

> It is on every ground of the highest importance that a sustained effort should be made to place elementary education in Egypt on a sound footing. The schoolmaster is abroad in the land. We may wish him well, but no one who is interested in the future of the country should blind himself to the fact that his social advantage carries with it certain avoidable disadvantages. The process of manufacturing demagogues has, in fact, not only begun, but may be said to be well advanced. . . . High education cannot and ought not to be checked or discouraged. . . . But if it is to be carried out without danger to the state, the ignorance of the masses should be tempered *pari passu* with the intellectual advance of those who are destined to be their leaders. It is neither wise nor just that the people should be left intellectually defenceless in the presence of the hare-brained and empirical projects which the political charlatan, himself but half-educated, will not fail to pour into their credulous ears.[34]

In terms of its imperial intent, Cromer's strategy was to use education as an instrument of both emulation, in the sense that a basic, limited, restricted elementary education would be offered to the masses to keep them culturally and politically compliant, and distant, in the sense that an educated Egyptian elite was to be restricted to avoid possible nationalistic consequences. In his study of Egyptian education, Bill Williamson sees the motives of Cromer's policy as

> to raise the level of education in village schools; . . . to create an efficient civil service; . . . to limit access to secondary and higher

education to avoid creating a group of people whose education, as he [Cromer] puts it 'unfits them for manual labour' so that they look exclusively to the government for labour; and, finally, to encourage technical education.[35]

Fundamental to this strategy was to approach an English teacher training college that could help train promising young Egyptian students in the complexities of modern elementary education so that they could help develop an efficient elementary education system in Egypt. The man chosen to make initial contact was Dr Douglas Dunlop, a senior official in the Ministry of Education.[36] Dunlop, a dour Scot, had been educated as a teacher in a Scottish training college before becoming a missionary in Africa. He was determined to follow Cromer's wishes to the full and exercised what virtually all his contemporaries described as a vice-like control over Egyptian education. In 1889 he contacted the Foreign Office, asking if it would be possible to accommodate two or three Egyptian students at an English training college. The Foreign Office contacted HMI Oakley,[37] the Chief Inspector of Training Colleges, and he suggested Borough Road College as the most appropriate institution for such an initiative.[38] Dunlop visited the college and had negotiations with Alfred Bourne,[39] secretary of the British and Foreign School Society and P.A. Barnett,[40] principal of the college. One of the initial sticking points was the question of whether or not the students were to be resident in the college. It was an issue on which Barnett had strong views. In a passage of typical period ethnocentricity – caught so well on so many occasions, incidentally, by Mangan – he opined that if they were not resident

> In the first place, the three students would lose what would be the most valuable part of their training and what is certainly the main purpose in the minds of those promoting their sojourn in England – the constant and sympathetic social intercourse with young Englishmen. In the next place they would be particularly exposed to the temptations of a real city; and no one who knows anything of the oriental character, and of Egyptian character and society in particular, would want to hold himself responsible for the uprightness of his charges.[41]

Barnett's views are illuminating for three reasons. In the first place they show that he and others readily acknowledged the importance of the impact of the socialization afforded by boarding, an important aspect of sound imperial and cultural transmission. Secondly, there is the tone of patronizing superiority in the attitude to the implied moral weakness of the Asian or African male. These were people who needed the shield of basic British *decency* to protect them from the temptations of London! This was a reflection of the self-regarding importance of the inculcation of imperial values through the college curriculum – an integral element of moral imperialism. Finally there was the notion of salvation: the notion that Britain can act as a facilitator of human development. Thus the 'Egyptian experiment' can be seen to contain all three strands of Mangan's imperial educational models.

Eventually, the problems of accommodation were resolved and the Egyptians took up residency in 1889. Barnett saw that the scheme had great potential benefits for the college: 'I generally favour the idea of making the college a centre of professional training not exclusively directed to the supply of one class of teachers only.'[42] This training included subscription to the special English imperial offering – athleticism.[43]

The scheme was a great success. Whatever initial doubts Barnett may have had were quickly dispelled and he recorded: 'I think it my duty to say at the outset that they come to us exceedingly well prepared. . . . The English students welcomed them very cordially and seem to lose no opportunity of doing them kindness and showing them things worth seeing.' He continued: 'I record with great satisfaction that our guests take part in the college outdoor games. I am also able to say that their health generally has been very good.'[44] The three students, Hamdy, Fahmy and Mansoury, were very popular with the students. When they left in 1891, the editor of the *B's Hum*, the college magazine recorded:

> We hope that they will always think with pleasure on their stay amongst us, and carry away with them some of the sports etc., they have learnt here, as well as the ordinary instruction. We shall no doubt hear of cricket at Cairo, captained by Hamdy, with Fahmy as bowler, and football teams with Mansoury as centre forward or some such thing, and before long it will be a common occurrence to see Egyptian teams playing in England and *vice versa*.[45]

On their return to Cairo the three students were introduced to a number of important and influential figures in Egyptian education including the Minister for Education, Yacoub Pasha Artin, who had visited Borough

Road; the Minister for Public Works, Zaky Pasha; and the British Consul
General, the Earl of Cromer himself! This meeting demonstrates the
importance of the scheme in Egyptian and British eyes. The students
were, in the words of Moussa Hamdy, determined 'to do Borough Road
College justice and preserve its name',[46] and the success of the Egyptian
connection was not restricted to the original three students. In February
1893, a contributor to the *B's Hum* noted: 'Our three latest Egyptian
comrades . . . are beginning to settle down; we hope be as much at home
as the solid Jimmy, frolicsome Joe, or sly old Billy. They are quite keen
as sportsmen, and turn out with commendable regularity to frolic with
the sphere.'[47]

This Egyptian experiment went beyond the supply of students to the
college. On a number of occasions, as we have already noted, the
Egyptian Ministry of Education sent representatives to see the work of
Borough Road. In 1892, the Minister of Public Instruction visited the
college. 'Yacoob Artin Pacha,' the *B's Hum* remarked approvingly, 'is an
exceedingly accomplished man, and well known for his interest in
education. He left assurances behind that the B.R.C. is making its mark
effectively in Egypt.'[48] With all parties seemingly pleased with the
relationship developed between Borough Road and Egypt, it was no real
surprise when a lecturer from Borough Road, A.V. Houghton,[49] was
appointed to the post of principal of the Khedivieh School in Cairo.
Another imperial educator keen on promoting athleticism in empire can
thus be added to Mangan's list of proselytizers.

Unsurprisingly, Houghton had been educated in the classic public
school and 'Oxbridge' tradition. His academic pedigree (Eton and
Hertford College, Oxford) was perfect, although he had to be content
with an *aegrotat* degree. His appointment at Borough Road was part of
a symbiotic relationship whereby the college offered young graduates
experience of elementary education and they, in turn, helped develop
athleticism there, and gave the college the symbols of increased social
standing and status.[50] Indeed while at Borough Road, Houghton
enthusiastically immersed himself in the sporting life of the college,
among other things, buying and presenting a challenge cup for cross-
country running.

When Houghton took up his post as principal, he immediately
sought out the ex-Borough Road students. Together they established a
Cairo education society. Each year a report of their work was faithfully
recorded in the *B's Hum*, an action that helped to reinforce ties of loyalty

and commitment between the two colleges. The Cairo society decided to mark its friendship with Borough Road by setting aside

> a part of its funds for a prize to be presented to the sports club of the Borough Road College for the coming reunion competition. We hope that Principal Withers[51] [Barnett's successor] will be so kind as to accept our proposal which is a sign of our high esteem of the principal and the college staff and our sincere goodwill towards the B's.[52]

Houghton lost no time in developing the athletic side of school life at Khedivieh School. In 1899 he refereed a football match between the combined Egyptian schools and the First Cameron Highlanders.[53] In addition, he wrote a patriotic preface and introductory note for an anthology of English poetry for Egyptian schools. The volume, he explained,

> has been primarily and especially compiled for use in the government schools of Egypt . . . with the definite aim of setting before the Egyptian pupils specimens of English and poetry which may excite their interests and their liking, and at the same time, give them some tangible idea of the pre-eminent beauty of the English language in its poetical aspects.[54]

It was through men and media such as these that the central message of both athleticism and imperialism was transmitted to the government schools of Egypt and, as Mangan has demonstrated so well, other schools in colony and dominion. The anthology was an explicit attempt to control the curriculum, to influence what Egyptian boys learned and mould their responses into desirable outcomes of loyalty and affinity to Empire. However, it was not as successful as some other places. The relationships between teacher and pupil were not as close in Egyptian schools as they were in many metropolitan public schools. Indeed Tignor has written that 'The English teacher's attitude towards his Egyptian students was one of contempt and ill will. One Egyptian remarked in his memoirs that students in his class did not know the names of their teacher, nor he their names.'[55] As a result of this kind of attitude it is not difficult to see why athleticism found it difficult to take root in Egypt. Nevertheless, according to Cromer, enthusiasm for games-playing did have a benign effect, described in his *Annual Report* of 1903: 'A remarkable feature in recent developments in connection with both the Primary and Secondary schools is the growing popularity of physical exercises and physical recreation. The Egyptians as a race are somewhat inclined to sedentary pursuits, and until recent years, the educational system confirmed rather than corrected this tendency.'[56] Cromer provided the reason, as he saw it, for the change:

A few years ago, physical drill and English sports were introduced into the curriculum of the Government schools. The effect upon the physique and character of the pupils has been so manifestly beneficial that their advantages are now generally recognised, even in quarters where their introduction was, at first, opposed.[57]

In other regards, his educational policy was a failure. Far from winning over the Egyptian population to view Britain with something akin to warmth and affection, it had the opposite effect and only served to alienate many of them. Bowman, a senior administrator in the education department, was in no doubt that the blame should be laid firmly at Cromer's (and others') door. Describing the practice of separation in the schools and society generally between the British and the Egyptians he believed that 'this was thoroughly bad policy, quite apart from bad manners; and it is reasonable to suppose that many of the difficulties of the twentieth century could have been avoided or at least minimised if it had been otherwise. Certainly in the schools the results were disastrous.'[58] And he continued: 'It was in the schools that [nationalism] was chiefly fostered, and it was the students who led the demonstrations. School strikes became so widespread that they threatened, at one time, to make the government almost powerless.'[59]

It was to prove a supreme irony, but by no means untypical in empire, that one of the Egyptian scholars selected under Cromer's scheme was to become one of the leading members for the movement for Egyptian independence. Shaik 'Abdul' Aziz Shawish had been appointed as an inspector in government schools after his return from Borough Road. He left the Ministry of Education to follow a career in politics and he told Bowman, with whom he had become friendly, that he was going to fight for independence. 'His frankness was disarming,' recalled Bowman:

'I intend to spend the rest of my life attacking the English,' he said. 'I have no quarrel with them personally and I have a number of English friends. But I want to see an independent Egypt, and I am determined to do all I can to make her so.'[60]

'The functional character of British education,' writes Williamson, 'was its hall mark, and the implementation of a strictly utilitarian education policy did much to galvanise nationalist opinion to the occupation itself and ensure that it was the educated classes and students which would emerge as the strongest oppositional force in Egypt.'[61] All this was quite typical, of course, of the indigenous middle-class response in empire to imperialism. They had the effective erudition and the educated confidence to oppose the foreign rulers.

Egypt was to prove a special case in the diffusion of imperialism. Its very history and relationship firstly, as part of the Ottoman empire, and subsequently the empires of France and Britain, ensured *ipso facto* that imperialism's evolution and diffusion was rather different from other imperial territories. The Earl of Cromer was determined to resist the rise of Egyptian nationalism as far as he could, while at the same time he publicly stated that it was government policy to withdraw from the country as soon as possible. It was to prove a difficult circle to square. Cromer's policy of offering only a functionalist curriculum in government schools was doomed to failure. Wealthy Egyptian families sent their sons to be educated in Europe, while the policy of sending some scholars to Borough Road to learn more about British elementary education had, in at least one case, the effect of aiding nationalist aspirations.

Paradoxically, given its long overseas associations, Borough Road may have been the least sensible training college to which to send Egyptian scholars. Although it was recognized as being pre-eminent in the field of elementary education, it had always enjoyed a Nonconformist and independent tradition.[62] It was also undergoing an educational renaissance. For the first time it was opening its doors to staff with public-school and university education. For these reasons it was less, rather than more, likely to be a breeding-ground for the type of educationists that Cromer desired. The vast majority of men at Borough Road were Nonconformist in background, had struggled against the odds to get a tertiary education and were now brought into contact with those who had enjoyed every educational advantage. They would probably have rejected Cromer's vision. As such, therefore, while athleticism may have been relatively easy to export through the medium of the training colleges, imperialism may have proved more difficult.

This state of affairs has been well discussed by Mangan. He makes the point, as do others less fully and certainly less fluently, that the British imperial legacy includes, in large measure, the creation by individualistic as well as conformist pioneers, of a twentieth-century peaceful, global, recreational revolution: the growth of modern sport as part of the globalization process, with all its vast ramifications – politically, culturally and so on. Thus, while British imperialism retreated, British cultural imperialism expanded and in Egypt the fact remains that the colleges were instruments of imperial athletic diffusion; yet their role in this process remains almost completely forgotten or ignored. This will certainly be put right. Mangan has acted as the pathfinder and pathmaker for others to follow. Perhaps it is appropriate to recall the lines of the Roman poet Lucretius (94–55BC):

> *Et quasi cursors vitai lampada tradunt*
> (And like runners pass on the torch of life)

CONCLUSION

It comes to few historians to have the wit, guile, freshness of approach or, if it does not seem sycophantic, brilliance to offer to others an entirely new dimension in historical writing. Taking the British public-school system as his theme, a phenomenon that has been the subject of hundreds of books, Mangan has opened a completely new window for us to look through. At the same time, he has encouraged others to look afresh through the window and scrutinize the impact and importance of athleticism in imperial, educational, social and cultural history. His writings on imperialism have challenged the pedantry of the past. He has successfully demonstrated that those who have simply regurgitated the historical and social shibboleths of yesteryear are doing themselves or their subject no favours. History is a dynamic, vibrant, challenging and constantly evolving discipline. As such it needs to be refreshed and re-stimulated by conceptual and empirical 'pathmakers and pathfinders'. And it is in this sense that Professor Mangan can rightly be awarded the accolade of a leader in historical studies.

NOTES

1. J.A. Mangan and John Nauright (eds), *Sport in Australian Society* (London and Portland, OR: Frank Cass, 2000); J.A. Mangan (ed.), *'Benefits Bestowed'?: Education and British Imperialism* (Manchester: Manchester University Press, 1988); J.A. Mangan and Paul Staudohar (eds), *Business of Professional Sports* (London: Frank Cass, 1991); J.A. Mangan (ed.), *The Cultural Bond: Sport, Empire, Society* (London: Frank Cass, 1992); J.A. Mangan, Richard Holt and Pierre Lanfranchi (eds), *European Heroes: Myth, Identity, Sport* (London and Portland, OR:

Frank Cass, 1996); J.A. Mangan and Roberta J. Park (eds), *From 'Fair Sex' to Feminism: Sport and the Socialization of Women in the Industrial and Post-industrial Eras* (London: Frank Cass, 1987); J.A. Mangan (ed.), *The Imperial Curriculum: Racial Images and Education in British Colonial Experience* (London: Frank Cass, 1993); J.A. Mangan, *Making Imperial Mentalities: Socialization and British Imperialism* (London: Frank Cass, 1990); J.A. Mangan (ed.), *Making European Masculinities: Sport, Europe, Gender* (*The European Sports History Review*, 2) (London and Portland, OR: Frank Cass, 2000); J.A. Mangan (ed.), *Sport in Europe: Politics, Class, Gender* (*The European Sports History Review*, 1) (London and Portland, OR: Frank Cass, 1999); J.A. Mangan (ed.), *Europe, Sport, World: Shaping Global Societies* (*The European Sports History Review*, 3 (London and Portland, OR: Frank Cass, 2001); J.A. Mangan and James Walvin, *Manliness and Morality: Middle-class Masculinity in Britain and America, 1800–1940* (London: Frank Cass, 1987); J.A. Mangan and Henrik Meinander (eds), *The Nordic World: Sport in Society* (London and Portland, OR: Frank Cass, 1998); J.A. Mangan (ed.), *Pleasure, Profit, Proselytism: British Culture and Sport at Home and Abroad, 1700–1914* (London: Frank Cass, 1988); J.A. Mangan (ed.), *Shaping the Superman: Fascist body as Political Icon – Aryan Fascism* (London and Portland, OR: Frank Cass, 1999); J.A. Mangan (ed.), *Significant Social Revolution: Cross-cultural Aspects of the Evolution of Compulsory Education* (London: Frank Cass, 1994); J.A. Mangan and William J. Baker (eds), *Sport in Africa: Essays in Social History* (London: Frank Cass, 1987); J.A. Mangan (ed.), *Superman Supreme: Fascist Body as Political Icon – Global Fascism* (London and Portland, OR: Frank Cass, 2000); J.A. Mangan, *Tribal Identities: Nationalism, Europe, Sport* (London and Portland, OR: Frank Cass, 1996); J.A. Mangan (ed.), *Sport, Culture, Society: International, Historical and Sociological Perspectives: Proceedings of the VIII Commonwealth and International Conference on Sport, Physical Education, Dance, Recreation, and Health 1986* (London: Spon,1986); J.A. Mangan, *Athleticism in the Victorian and Edwardian Public School: The Emergence and Consolidation of an Educational Ideology* (London and Portland, OR: Frank Cass, 2000); James A. Mangan, *The Games Ethic and Imperialism: Aspects of the Diffusion of an Ideal* (London and Portland, OR: Frank Cass, 1998); J.A. Mangan, *Physical Education and Sport: Sociological and Cultural Perspectives, An Introductory Reader* (Oxford: Basil Blackwell, 1973).

2. Jeffrey Richards, 'Introduction', in Mangan, *Athleticism*, p.xxiv.
3. S. Rothblatt, 'Foreword', in Mangan, *Athleticism*, p.xix.
4. Mangan, *The Games Ethic*, p.19.
5. Mangan, *'Benefits Bestowed'?*, p.2.
6. George H. Nadel and Perry Curtis, *Imperialism and Colonialism* (London: Macmillan, 1966), quoted in Mangan, *'Benefits Bestowed'?*, p.1.
7. Ibid., p.2.
8. Ibid., pp.3–4.
9. Ibid.
10. Ibid., p.5.
11. Harold Silver, *Education as History* (London: Methuen, 1983), p.3.
12. Mangan, *'Benefits Bestowed'?*, pp.16–17.
13. Joan Simon, 'The History of Education in Past and Present', *Oxford Review of Education*, 3, 1 (1977), 71.
14. Ibid.
15. Mangan, *'Benefits Bestowed'?*, p.18.
16. J.A. Mangan (ed.), *Making Imperial Mentalities*, p.1.
17. Ibid., p.2. See also Barrie Stacey, *Political Socialization in Western Society* (London: Edward Arnold, 1978), p.3.
18. Mangan, *Making Imperial Mentalities*, p.2.
19. Ibid.
20. Ibid. See also Edward M. Bruner, 'Cultural Transmission and Cultural Change', *Southwestern Journal of Anthropology*, 12 (1956), pp.191–9.
21. Mangan, *Making Imperial Mentalities*, p.3.
22. Ibid. See also Rene Maunier, *The Sociology of Colonies: An Introduction to the Study of Race Contact* (ed. and trans. E. O. Lorimer), Vol.2 (London: Routledge & Kegan Paul, 1949), p.425.
23. A.L. Kroeber and C. Kluckhohn, 'Culture: A Critical Review of Concepts and Definitions',

Papers of the Peabody Museum of American Archaeology and Ethnology, 70 (1952), 227.

24. Mangan, *The Cultural Bond*, p.1.
25. Ibid.
26. Patrick Bratlinger, *Rites of Darkness: British Literature and Imperialism* (Ithaca, NY, 1988), p. 15.
27. Clifford Gertz, *The Interpretation of Cultures* (New York, 1973), p.218.
28. Mangan, *The Cultural Bond*, p.6.
29. See for example, J.A. Mangan and Colm Hickey, 'English Elementary Education Revisited and Revised: Drill and Athleticism in Tandem', in Mangan, *Sport in Europe*, pp.63–91; J.A. Mangan and Colm Hickey, 'Athleticism in the Service of the Proletariat: Preparation for the English Elementary School and the Extension of Middle-Class Manliness', in Mangan, *Making European Masculinities*, pp.112–39; J.A. Mangan and Colm Hickey, 'Globalization, the Games Ethic and Imperialism: Further Aspects of the Diffusion of an Ideal', in Mangan, *Europe, Sport, World*, pp.105–30; and J.A. Mangan and Colm Hickey, 'A Pioneer of the Proletariat: Herbert Milnes and the Games Cult in New Zealand', in Mangan and Nauright, *Sport in Australasian Society*, pp.31–48.
30. Lawrence James, *The Rise and Fall of the British Empire* (London: Abacus Books, 1994), p.272.
31. Ibid., p.271.
32. R. Shannon, *The Crisis of Imperialism* (London: Granada, 1976), p.159.
33. Evelyn Baring (1841–1917) entered Woolwich in 1855. He spent the next 20 years as an officer in Malta, Greece and Jamaica. In 1883 he was appointed consul-general of Egypt. He was made Baron Cromer in 1892, viscount in 1899 and earl in 1901. He was the author of *Modern Egypt* (London: Macmillan, 1908), *Ancient and Modern Imperialism* (London: John Murray, 1910), *Abbas II* (London: Macmillan, 1915), and three volumes of *Political and Literary Essays* (London: Macmillan, 1912).
34. Earl of Cromer, *Modern Egypt* (London: Macmillan, 1908), Vol.2, p.534.
35. B. Williamson, *Education and Social Change in Egypt and Turkey. A study in Historical Sociology* (London: Macmillan, 1987), p.79.
36. Douglas Dunlop (1860–19??) was born in Glasgow. He was a pupil at Overnewton Public School and studied at Glasgow University from 1878 to 1885. He gained an M.A. degree in 1883 and was awarded an Honorary degree of Director of Laws in 1898 as a result of his appointment as Secretary-General of the Department of Public Instruction in Cairo, a post he held until his retirement in 1923. One of his colleagues recalled: 'He was undoubted a man of ability and industry. But his horizon was limited by his narrow upbringing, and his aim was to produce in the schools of the Egyptian Government efficiency based on rigid uniformity and iron discipline.' H. Bowman, *Middle-East Window* (London: Longmans, 1942), p.42.
37. Henry Evelyn Oakley (1835–1915), the third son of Sir Herbert Oakley, Bart. was educated at Rugby and Jesus College, Cambridge, where he was a 10th Wrangler, taking his B.A. in 1859 and his M.A. in 1862. He was made a Fellow of Jesus College in 1860. He was a H.M.I., 1864–78 and Chief Inspector of Training Colleges, 1885–99. He was knighted in 1915.
38. Borough Road College was, arguably, the most prestigious training college in England and Wales at this time. It had been founded in 1798 by Joseph Lancaster and, as it was administered by the British and Foreign School Society, had a long tradition of working with students from overseas. A significant number of men trained at Borough Road went on to work in a host of schools, colleges and universities in the empire. For a history of the college see G.F. Bartle, *A History of Borough Road College* (Kettering: Dalkeith Press, 1976). For a consideration of athleticism and imperialism in the college see C.F. Hickey, 'Athleticism and the Training Colleges: The Proletarian Absorption of an Educational Ideology' (unpublished PhD thesis, University of Strathclyde, 2002). For the impact of some former students in empire see Mangan and Hickey, 'Globalization, the Games Ethic and Imperialism' and Mangan and Hickey, 'A Pioneer of the Proletariat'.
39. Alfred Bourne (1832–1907) was born in London and educated at Stockwell Grammar School and set up a private school in Clapham. He trained as a Congregational minister and graduated from the University of London in 1855. After missionary work in the West Indies he became secretary of the British and Foreign School Society in 1868.
40. P.A. Barnett (1858–1941) was born in London and educated at City of London School and

Trinity College, Oxford. He then became professor of English at Firth College, Sheffield. He was principal of Borough Road from 1889 to 1893, when he left to join the education inspectorate from 1893 to 1918, during which time he was made Assistant Inspector of Training Colleges and spent a two-year secondment as Superintendent of Education for Natal. He was the Chief Inspector for Training Colleges from 1905 to 1918 and Civil Adviser for the War Office on Army education from 1919-21. He published *Teaching and Organisation* (1897), *Common Sense in Education* (1899), *The Story of Robinson Crusoe in Latin* (1906) and *Common Sense Grammar* (1923). He later became chairman of the Board of Governors at Borough Road in 1929.

41. 'Memorandum regarding the request made by the Egyptian Administration for permission to place three Egyptians Students at the Borough Road College', Barnett Papers 405, British and Foreign School Society Archives.

42. Ibid., p.2.

43. See Mangan, *Athleticism*, *passim* for the authoritative outline of this educational ideology.

44. 'Egyptian Students', Barnett Papers 405, p.1.

45. *B's Hum*, III, 23 (Oct. 1891), 143–4.

46. *B's Hum*, IV, 25 (Feb. 1892), 2–3.

47. *B's Hum*, V, 35 (Feb.–March 1893), 2.

48. *B's Hum*, IV, 30 (Aug.–Sept. 1892), 5.

49. Arthur Villiers Houghton (1872–19??) was born in Boston Spa, Yorkshire, the son of the Revd E.J. Houghton. He was educated at Eton and Hertford College, Oxford, from 1890 to 1892 with an Abbots Scholarship in 1891 and Classical Moderations in 1892, being awarded an *aegrotat* degree (given to those who missed their finals through illness).

50. For a fuller discussion of this point see C.F. Hickey, 'Athleticism and the Training College': The Proletarian Absorprion of an Educational Ideology', Ch.3.

51. H.A. Withers (1864–1903) was educated at King's School, London, and Balliol College, Oxford, where he took a first in Classical Greats. He then became housemaster at Clifton College before his appointment as principal of Borough Road in 1893, a post he held until 1900, when he became professor of education at Owen's College, Manchester.

52. *B's Hum*, X, 82 (Jan. 1899), 24.

53. *B's Hum*, X, 83 (Feb. 1899), 2.

54. G. Cookson, *English Poetry for Schools* (London: Macmillan, 1899), p.vii.

55. Robert L. Tignor, *Modernisation and British Colonial Rule in Egypt 1882–1914* (Princeton, NJ: Princeton University Press, 1966), p.328.

56. *Cromer Report* (1903), Cd.1951, p.61.

57. Ibid.

58. H. Bowman, *Middle East Window* (London: Longmans, 1942), p.42.

59. Ibid.

60. Ibid., p.77.

61. Williamson, *Education and Social Change*, p.81.

62. The college was widely respected in the educational community, with its vice-principal, Joshua Fitch (later knighted) becoming Chief HMI for women's training colleges. In 1893, Barnett also joined the inspectorate. In 1895 a visiting inspector wrote of the staff that he considered it 'the strongest of any college I have yet come across'. For a consideration of the college's standing see G.F. Bartle, 'Staffing Policy at a Victorian Training College', *Victorian Education* (History of Education Society Occasional Publication), 2 (Summer 1976), pp.14–23.

6

Pointing the Way – Antipodean Responses to J.A. Mangan's *Athleticism* and Related Studies: Scotch College, Melbourne, in the Inter-war Years

MARTIN CROTTY

Only the churlish could deny that J.A. Mangan's *Athleticism in the Victorian and Edwardian Public School* was a seminal work. With acute insight Mangan illustrated how public-school headmasters, supported by a range of assistants and employing methods ranging from compulsory games to execrable verse, established the practice, rhetoric and ideology of the games field as the central pillar of England's middle- and upper-class learning institutions. In conjunction with David Newsome, Norman Vance and others, Mangan illustrated a shifting educational focus, away from the mind and the spirit of the pupil towards his body and his character.[1] The genius of his work is reflected by the fact that it become an essential text for historians of sport, of education and of masculinity – and, to a lesser degree, to historians of class and of the British Empire.

Athleticism was principally about the formulation and dissemination to its subjects of a dominant, or hegemonic, ideology. Mangan does, to his credit, illustrate occasions where the hegemony was resisted. The diary of Samuel Roebuck, for example, documents his increasing dismay at the introduction of compulsory games at Lancing in the years from 1860 to 1862. As Mangan points out, sickness, real or imagined, absence, non-cooperation or other strategies could be, and were, employed by the unfit or the unenthusiastic. If they wanted to read rather than run, to bask rather than bowl, or to work rather than wrestle, a range of tactics would often allow them to fashion counter-hegemonic existences within the dominant ideology.[2] Nonetheless, it is fair to say that Mangan's principal concern was with the way boys were supposed to behave, rather than with what they actually experienced.

Mangan's basic approach of focusing on dominant ideas and how they sought to suppress subversive ones has informed the work of most of those who have built on his findings, whether they be writing in the fields of sports history, educational history or gender history – or indeed where the three intersect. In his introduction to his edited volume *Pleasure, Profit, Proselytism: British Culture and Sport at Home and Abroad 1700–1914*, Mangan himself summed up the range of essays and the themes they considered. The contributors were concerned, he said,

> most importantly with the role of sport in the establishment and maintenance of class-consciousness, and as a corollary, in the creation and reinforcement of class differences at home and abroad; with sport not only as a source of tension, as one writer has put it, outstripping the reach of existing systems of social control, but also as an intended instrument of hegemonic influence utilized in self-assured attempts to achieve adherence to middle-class metropolitan values; and finally, and paradoxically, with sport as a means of establishing virtually simultaneously class, national and imperial unities.[3]

Similarly, John Hargreaves has, in his analysis of popular sports in Britain, focused on how working-class sports and their associated values of licentiousness, riotousness and drunkenness (with sporting 'carnivals' acting as a kind of 'charivari' where the world could temporarily be turned upside down) were gradually suppressed in favour of middle-class sports and their associated values of amateurism, fair play, order, rationality and moral purpose.[4] In gender terms, Hargreaves states that reconstructed sports 'became a major source of male identity and a major basis for gender division' whereby men confirmed their difference from, and dominance over, women.[5]

This is the analysis of sport as a hegemonic influence; used to bring imperial peoples, lower classes and the young into supporting a dominant male, middle-class and metropolitan world view. There have been a few exceptions of course, but the emphasis on the constitution and dissemination of the hegemonic has been pronounced and robust.[6] This basic approach has been replicated in Australian treatments of sport, particularly with regard to sport and education. David Brown, Bob Stewart, David Kirk and I have all looked at the Antipodean versions of athleticism and how the use of sports in Australia's elite schools become one of the main pillars supporting the schools' efforts to inculcate 'manliness' into their charges.[7] Where the analysis has had a gender focus, the main emphases have been on how Australian sport has been used to reinforce patriarchal gender relations or, alternatively, how sport has been used to privilege and endorse one construction of masculinity over another – what Bob Connell has called the establishment of a 'hegemonic masculinity'.[8]

Few, however, have considered the lived experience of masculinity or the reception of ideology; how young men actually responded and reacted to their schooling and the messages presented to them in the process. There has been an implicit assumption that boys in schools are empty vessels, passive recipients of the meanings of manliness and masculinity presented to them in the rhetoric of their masters, in the symbols and language of their surroundings, in the ethics of the games field and in the writings of ideologues. There are enough instances of boys applying peer pressure to others to force them to conform to the prevailing ideals, and enough signs of acquiescence, such as the widespread enthusiasm for (not just acceptance of) games and the tragically willing response of old boys to the outbreak of hostilities in 1914, for us to be confident that the ideological messages presented to boys fell on fertile soil. But there were 'shirkers' and 'loafers', 'stewpots' and aesthetes. The constant harping of headmasters about the need to be rid of these 'fatted sows' testifies to their continued presence, while occasions of boyhood vandalism of school property bear witness to the ability of boys to protest against their superiors even when more legitimate avenues of challenge had been closed off or had proved fruitless.[9]

Accessing boys' lived experience of masculinity, their schooling and their experience of athleticism presents a number of practical and methodological difficulties. Boys did not record their views on such matters with such readiness as did their schoolmasters, and even letters home to parents were likely to have been heavily censored, if not by domineering masters then by the boys themselves. We do not have access to the kinds of fine collections of letters and diaries that allowed Margot Fry, in an impressive recent book, to analyse how Tom King experienced and dealt with ideas of masculinity as a young gentleman seeking his fortune in New Zealand.[10]

Memoirs of time at school go some way towards solving this problem. Recollections and reflection are brought together, and we can see how the ideological messages and methods helped to shape individuals' sense of themselves and the world around them. They are, however, not without methodological challenges as sources. The writers of memoirs are not, for example, a representative grouping. By definition, most of those who wrote memoirs went on to live lives worth recording. For every old boy who led such a life, there were dozens of others who led unexceptional existences, making their way without making an impact. Are memoir writers thus likely to have happier recollections of their schooldays as they were able to make enough success of their later lives to deem memoirs worth writing? Perhaps, but the opposite might also be true. It could be argued that to lead their exceptional lives, these boys would have had to develop critical faculties and levels of initiative that would have sat ill at ease with the conformist orientation of schools, thus making them more critical of their schooldays. For each one of these, one might speculate, there were probably dozens of others who went quietly, contentedly and unquestioningly on their way. It might also be argued that the types of old boy who possessed both the capability and willingness to write books about their lives were more likely to have been the literary aesthetes of their schools, thus recalling a frequently hostile environment. It is vital to remember that the contented boy who played and adored sport, who imbibed the ideology of manliness fostered by the elite schooling system and who went on to live an unexceptional life marked by solid employment and secure family, would be unlikely to possess the life experiences to make recollections worth writing, let alone publishing or reading. Nonetheless, recollections provide a window onto the pasts of some individuals, and allow us to form a vision, albeit a distorted one at times, of how schooling was experienced; not just how it was supposed to be experienced.

Scotch College, Melbourne, was a Presbyterian establishment founded in 1851. Along with Wesley College, Melbourne Grammar School, Geelong Grammar School, Geelong College and Xavier College, it formed Victoria's elite secondary system of 'public' schools based on English precedent, employing English masters and mimicking English public-school ideology. Through the late nineteenth and the early twentieth century, these schools gradually shifted their educational emphasis away from religion and intellectualism towards athleticism, 'character' and militarism. There were, to be sure, differences in the timing of the ideological shift. The charge was led by Geelong Grammar and Wesley College, while Scotch and Xavier were relative laggards, showing less enthusiasm for the practices and trappings of athleticism in particular, due to their religious and ethnic inheritances and to the personalities of the men who controlled them. By early in the twentieth century, however, the ideologies these schools subscribed to and the methods they employed were remarkably uniform, a uniformity resulting, in part, from the narrowing of religious differences in Australia, the overwhelming spirit of militarism and the replacement of some key personalities. In Scotch's case, Alexander Morrison died in office and was replaced by W.S. Littlejohn in 1904, a man who showed considerably more enthusiasm for the trappings of the English public-school system, such as games and prefects, than had his predecessor. The essential, shared ideal was that the public school product should be patriotic, fit, selfless and ethical. He should know how to 'play the game'. Scholastic learning has since returned as a central educational goal; militarism has faded after the horrors of the First World War and its deadly toll on so many old boys, and religion has waxed and waned. In this elite educational system, however, the emphasis on character has remained central, and none of the elite six has rested content with intellectual training.[11] Schools such as Scotch have boasted of their old boys and their achievements, and have claimed a major part in their training, fitting them for their achievements through an 'all-round' education embodying the intellectual, the physical and the spiritual, but always with 'character' as a central plank.

The gap between the self-proclaimed mission of the schools and the self-recalled experience of boys – the gulf between the dissemination and reception of educational ideology – is, however, marked. Using the most recent history of Scotch College as a guide (James Mitchell's monumental *A Deepening Roar*), I have been able to identify nine authors who wrote extensively of Scotch in their memoirs. Only one was unambiguously fond of his Scotch College time; the remainder varied from cynical to explicitly and relentlessly hostile. Moreover, few referred to the lofty goals of the school, and sport rated the barest of mentions, or no mention at all, in a number of cases. Clearly, self-selected group that they might be, writers of memoirs understood their time at school in terms vastly different from those intended by headmasters and others. The widely varying reactions boys had to their schooling is evidenced by the writings of five old boys, all at Scotch in the 1920s. Archibald Glenn, Graham McInnes, Ross Campbell, David McNicol and Alan Moorehead tell very different stories of the same school, their widely varying reactions serving to illustrate the different possibilities for the reception of school ideology, and different strategies for coping with it.

Of all the memoirs, only those of Archibald Glenn, *Things to be Remembered*, provide a ringing endorsement of Scotch. Glenn was indeed a Scotch success story in his years there from 1927 to 1929: he was a member of the first rowing eight for two years and Captain of the Boats for one (rowing was the elite sport of the elite Victorian schools), won a scholarship to Melbourne University and another to Ormond College, became a prominent industrialist, was the first Chancellor of Melbourne's La Trobe University and was eventually knighted. He also spent 29 years on the Scotch College council, 19 of them as chairman. It is not surprising, in the circumstances, that he recalls his time at Scotch College fondly: 'The full life at Scotch gave me an opportunity I was lucky enough to be able to take.'[12] Glenn recalls Littlejohn as 'one of my prime heroes',[13] and emphasizes his contribution to Scotch sport: 'How lucky I was in my brief three years at Scotch to have the privilege of knowing him. He was always interested in the school crew and he enjoyed coming down to the river to watch us training and to chat afterwards.'[14]

Glenn also defends Scotch against a familiar charge; that of being elitist, out of tune with the broader egalitarian ethos of Australian society:

> People often talk glibly about Scotch being an elite school. My experience of it was that of fine middle-class people who came from homes where the old virtues of chivalry, loyalty, and help and understanding for the less privileged were still paramount. If this is being elite, then so be it. The world has made great strides since I was a schoolboy but a lot of people have lost the old virtues of consideration for others.[15]

Sport looms large in Glenn's recollections – he talks in detail of his rowing experiences and many of his rowing friends who later became business associates.

Glenn's story is almost directly in accordance with how the Scotch College ideologues would have envisaged the path of a successful schoolboy and old boy. Academic success is mixed with sporting achievement. The values of camaraderie and social service shine through, and he goes on to a distinguished career. The icing on the cake is Glenn's return to the college as a member of the board of governors;

contributing selflessly to the former school whose ideals he has lived by and still seeks to uphold. He was a willing recipient of early twentieth-century public-school ideology; imbibing it, living by it and serving to further it.

Less enamoured with Scotch, but also something of a success story, is Graham McInnes. Educated at Scotch in the 1920s, McInnes, like Glenn, went on to enjoy a successful career, most notably as a diplomat and writer. In three volumes of memoirs, respectively titled *The Road to Gundagai*, *Humping my Bluey* and *Goodbye Melbourne Town*, which often cover the same ground, McInnes is at his most revealing in his portrayals of the masters, the boys and the relationships between them, in all cases seeing them, if not as intolerable, then certainly as flawed.

McInnes recalls the headmaster, Littlejohn, and his deputy with some affection, as appropriate in the public-school world where boys were expected to look up to and respect their masters. 'Old Bill', as the headmaster was known, was held in awe, and was considered 'a just man' despite occasionally being severe – 'in a crisis we would be fairly, if harshly, dealt with'.[16] 'Bumpy' Ingram, the vice-principal, is also recalled fondly, particularly for his habit, when cricket matches were on, of allowing a boy 'to stand at the window and repeat the score at one minute intervals'.[17] Collectively, McInnes recalls the masters as being a big influence on the boys in their charge, and generally a benevolent one:

> Together, under Old Bill Littlejohn and Bumpy Ingram, they formed a hierarchy of the freeborn in which ramming it into a boy was balanced by a nice sense of getting it out of him. Certainly, for good or ill, the ten years spent with them were bound to be the most formative of a boy's life.[18]

The constant exhortations to boys to do better, to make more of themselves, to try harder, were reflected in schoolboy rivalries, McInnes recalls. From a Scotch College perspective, Geelong Grammar was untouchable, the elite of the elite, the school where the wealthy squatters of the Western District sent their sons.[19] Wesley College, as a Methodist school, was mocked for being a collection of 'wowsers', and Wesley boys met in the streets would be jeered with lines such as 'Wesley wowsers wet their trousers', while the Catholic Xaverians would be treated to 'Catholic dogs jump like frogs'.[20] Melbourne Grammar School, however, viewed by Scotch boys as snobs ('Who-ah? We-ah! Melbahn Grammah!') were the fiercest rivals of all, perhaps with an element of

Anglo-Celtic rivalry. Fights between supporters at football matches were apparently common, and victory was never sweeter than when achieved over the more pretentious cousins in their older quarters closer to the city centre.

McInnes was more interested in singing and in plays than he was in sport, but clearly still imbibed elements of the athletic ideology and the rivalry between the elite schools that helped to foster and maintain the Victorian games system. There is little enough in all of this that the masters would have objected to – they encouraged the rivalry, partly out of their own competitive spirits, partly because it motivated boys to try harder, and partly because sporting successes added to school prestige and translated into growing enrolments. Moreover, the fact that McInnes was able to enjoy the school rivalries even though more interested in drama and music provides some evidence that the emphasis on games was not completely exclusive of other interests. The ideal was that boys could excel in a number of fields, and the rhetoric of the Victorian public schools in the pre-war and post-war periods suggests that by the 1920s what had been an almost total obsession with games and militarism had weakened somewhat, allowing boys to pursue more diverse interests. Notably, the *Scotch Collegian* frequently asserted that the current age 'was tending too much to become an age of athleticism' and that an overemphasis on sporting success could 'belittle the importance of School work and the various other activities of School life'.[21] McInnes's recollections provide further evidence that this was indeed the case. Postwar the schools could accommodate, even within a continuing games cult, a broader range of interests than had hitherto been possible.

Nonetheless, McInnes's memoirs also illustrate a darker side to school existence. Relations between masters and boys were not always as paternal and respectful as the characterization of 'Old Bill' Littlejohn might suggest. McInnes also recalls Sergeant Cartwright, a bullying drillmaster who enjoyed the cruel display of matching the strong against the weak in the boxing ring, and Armitage, 'the real sadist of the school', who 'hit boys with such force that they flew from their seat'.[22] Not that the boys did not on occasion bring such treatment on themselves, or at least contribute to it. McInnes also recalls 'the refined cruelty whereby an unpopular master was mercilessly lynched, tarred and feathered', the boys so provoking one master that he took an enormous swing at one boy with a closed fist, fortunately not connecting, before Littlejohn appeared on the scene to calm matters.[23]

Although no devotee of athletic pursuits himself, McInnes recalls Scotch as heavily influenced by the competitive rivalry of the games field, and he, like most of his fellows, held the school's top athletes in awe. Of the unintellectual captain of the school, who once instructed prefects to bring 'six spatchelors' to assist in the school's then customary medical inspections, McInnes remembers:

> He was a sober, moderately inarticulate fellow of medium height and unassailable purity. Both his Homeric exploits and his natural modesty put us all to shame. He was a triple blue, Captain of Cricket and Captain of Football as well as being Captain of School; yet all this eminence failed to keep from his face, beneath its thick eaves of taw-coloured hair, a faint form of puzzlement. Perhaps his skill in the field, while matched by his sterling character, somewhat outran his other capacities.[24]

The note of ambivalence in McInnes's recollections is probably due to his apparently being clever enough to pursue non-athletic interests and to see the limitations of athleticism, but at the same time accepting enough of the prevailing ideology of the school to form such an admiration for the non-intellectual qualities of the school's captain.

The positive aspect of his memories may also be attributable to McInnes's successes at the school. Although not an athlete of note, McInnes performed well academically, which, along with the longevity of his attendance and his presumably good character, prompted Littlejohn to make him a prefect for 1929. Prefect status, and the badge that indicated it, conferred esteem among one's fellows and among the girls with whom McInnes and other Scotch Collegians travelled on the tram. Notes could be passed to the young ladies of Methodist Ladies' College or Presbyterian Ladies' College on the back of a 'Scholar's Concession Check', though McInnes recalls this as a hazardous practice as the note could be refolded en route to read 'Scholar's Cock'. As well as the special badges, prefects had their own rooms, special privileges and rights, and were charged with assisting in enforcing the discipline of the school, a task they addressed with a sometimes sadistic relish.[25]

McInnes's positive experiences and successes, combined with the critical possibilities of distance and intelligence, lead to a tone of reserved fondness in his memoirs. Not a classic public-school product because of his lack of athleticism, he was nonetheless able to fashion an intellectual, artistic and prefectorial existence within the prevailing hegemony. So too did Ross Campbell, a contemporary of McInnes of similar inclination, albeit a little less successfully.

Campbell, who soon discovered that he completely lacked talent for sporting pursuits, was a self-confessed 'swot' who gained pleasure at school from the pursuit of academic achievement.[26] He also edited the *Scotch Collegian* for a period, his main extracurricular activity at Scotch. Like McInnes he performed well academically, well enough to win a scholarship to Melbourne University and another to Ormond College.[27]

But Campbell remained uninspired by the sporting and military activities of Scotch College, and never warmed to the character messages presented to him. Drill was simply a 'tiresome duty' that interrupted his 'agreeable existence' at Scotch. While 'a corporal expounded the incomprehensible workings of a "Looey" gun', Campbell 'lolled in boredom'.[28] Campbell's cynicism towards the extolled purposes of military training and his inability at sport were symptomatic and reflective of a broader lack of interest and enthusiasm for the wider ideological messages of the school, as clearly revealed in his recollections of a school speech day:

> The general told us our schooldays were the best days of our lives. He went on to hope that we would always fear God, shoot straight and honour the King.
>
> I was not sure that I believed in God. I did not like the bangs that accompanied shooting, and I had only a lukewarm regard for King George V. I listened impatiently for the speech to end. It did at last, and I took my place in the line of boys waiting for prizes.[29]

His lack of 'school spirit' continued at Ormond, a residential college at the University of Melbourne, where he was much less impressed than Archie Glenn at the initiation rituals: 'The system was kept going by gregarious fellows who believed in the team spirit. Many of us thought it a waste of time, but we put up with it and when it was over we were treated with camaraderie'.[30]

Nonetheless, Campbell too was able to carve out a niche within the overriding hegemony of 'heartiness'. By the 1920s the focus on athleticism had receded somewhat, and Campbell was not considered the 'loafer' or 'slacker' for his inability at sports that he might have been at, for example, L.A. Adamson's Wesley College. It is notable that he refers to 'my agreeable existence as a senior frog in the school pond', and if the heartiness of school spirit did little to inspire him, it was something he could bear while he awaited opportunities to pursue interests of his own choosing. Campbell excelled academically, won a Rhodes Scholarship to study at Oxford, and went on to become one of Australia's most well-known journalists. If uninspiring, Campbell's schooldays were, in his own memory, at least manageable.

The mixture of good and bad is further revealed in the memoirs of David McNicol, a pupil at Scotch from 1927 to 1932. *Luck's A Fortune: An Autobiography* reads similarly to the stories told by McInnes and Campbell, except that the horrors are magnified, the departures from what would have been considered 'appropriate' behaviour more extreme and the praise, almost paradoxically, more fulsome. McNicol was sent to Scotch by his father partly because of the high reputation enjoyed by the headmaster, Littlejohn, but McNicol 'found a considerable portion of my schooldays utter misery'.[31] Far from being the place of camaraderie and fellowship that it pronounced itself, McNicol initially found Scotch a place of lawlessness, a throwback to the brutal English public schools of the nineteenth century where the strong dominated the weak and the law of the jungle prevailed:

> My first term at the school was hellish. I was lonely, bewildered, bullied. The initiation system was in full swing in those days, and it was brutal. Needles stuck in the buttocks, running the gauntlet of rows of senior boys while they flicked at your bottom with wet towels, finding bedding soaked with water just before retiring, bootblack plastered on shirts, shoe laces removed from shoes, all the usual indignities and japes. Twelve months later I was in the ranks of the tormentors.
>
> Quite the most unpleasant initiation ceremony was to be compulsorily matched, bare fisted, against some fellow new-boy. These contests were held in the shower room, the elder boys lining the walls and shouting encouragement or threats at the contestants. As the penalty for running dead was several whacks across the backside from everyone present, the contestants learnt to throw everything they had into the fights. In my first encounter I finished a bloody mess, nose streaming gore, one eye closed. Not a master commented on my appearance.[32]

McNicol found life as a boarder at Scotch so horrendous that at the end of his first term, on returning home, he burst into tears and begged his parents not to send him back.

Mangan has written of the strong streak of social Darwinism that pervaded public school educational ideology in England in Victorian and Edwardian times.[33] David Brown, in his study of the memoirs of Canadian public schoolboys, has suggested that the same sort of thinking existed in Canada, where the institutionalized cruelty was part of a calculated attempt to breed hardiness into boys under an ideology that Brown terms 'Sparto-Christianity'.[34] Similar ideas seem to have existed at Scotch. Despite the rhetoric about fellowship, the *Scotch Collegian* gave considerable endorsement to the idea that peers and masters could, with a degree of ruthlessness, force boys to sink or swim:

> Awkward corners and mannerisms, peculiar ideas and customs are smoothed out by the purging fire of youthful criticism. The searchlight of a Public School is strong and ruthless; it brings out most of the weakness of a boy's character, but it also brings out its strength. A boy who can rise to one of the highest positions in the Public School possesses character.[35]

There is no explicit endorsement here of the sort of trial by fire to which McNicol was subjected, but the suggestion that boys had to make their own way, had to fight for survival and have their character tested goes a considerable way to explaining the benign neglect of the masters when boys such as McNicol clearly bore the scars of their initiation experiences.

McNicol of course, did survive, but his acquisition of 'school spirit' was not total. He never excelled at sport. Despite making the house athletics team and scraping into the tennis squad, he was 'pathetic' at cricket and football and never graduated beyond training boats in rowing, despite expressing some admiration for the quality of the school's sporting facilities. Nor apparently, was McNicol overly impressed by sporting ideology; not once in his memoirs does he mention the benefits of team work, self-discipline or selflessness – the qualities of 'manliness' that sport was supposed to play such a central part in developing.

Unlike others, McNicol remembers Littlejohn as being enthusiastic about sport, but as never letting the boys forget 'that he considered academic prowess of far more importance'.[36] And unlike others who recall second-rate masters, or who can remember little of their teaching, McNicol is full of praise for the academic side of the school. Scotch was, he says, 'blessed . . . with top calibre masters, many of them renowned in

the academic world. . . . They were men of humour and understanding.
. . . Nothing was ever a trouble, nothing too tedious to be explained
thoroughly to the slowest in the class . . . lessons became magic.'[37]
McNicol lauded Littlejohn especially, regarding him as the greatest
influence on his life by a distance.

McNicol was able to progress to the top ranks of the school,
eventually becoming a prefect after being invited back by Littlejohn to
do an honours year. Despite this, and despite a heavy involvement in
drama and literature, McNicol appears to have been selective about the
aspects of Scotch and Presbyterian ideology that he absorbed or adhered
to. Sport never meant much to him, and abstemious ideals of personal
purity appear to have passed him by. He recalls the delights of being
'introduced to the magical world of masturbation' and of losing his
virginity to 'a not unattractive prostitute in Little Lonsdale Street' in his
third or fourth year of boarding. Prefect status brought a number of
privileges, chief among them being that it was 'much easier to procure
the occasional bottle of hooch, and to sneak out to the races'.[38] Again,
hegemonic ideals were to be negotiated, not blindly accepted.

If McNicol, Campbell and McInnes were able to carve out tolerably
happy existences at Scotch by accepting aspects of the prevailing
ideology while rejecting others, Alan Moorehead's memoirs remind us
that this was not the case for all. Also at Scotch during the 1920s,
Moorehead was later to become a distinguished and prolific journalist,
writer and historian, perhaps best known for his 1957 book *Gallipoli*. But
years later Moorehead's recollections of his schooldays left him
'oppressed by sensations of frustration and despair'.[39] He was not, like
Glenn, a proficient sportsman, and unlike McNicol, Campbell and
McInnes was unable to trade on intellectual achievement to advance in
the school hierarchy or to win respect, however grudging, from his peers
or teachers. In Moorehead's own words:

> I had been a most unsuccessful schoolboy, invariably at the bottom
> of my class and unable to get into any of the teams, but this hardly
> explains the sense of loathing – yes, positive loathing – that still
> overcomes me whenever I think of that place. I attended the
> school as a day-boy for ten years, and surely there must have been
> pleasant episodes in all that time. Yet all I can remember now is
> those meaningless morning prayers, the heat of those
> overcrowded classrooms through the long droning afternoon,

those second-rate masters brought out from England with their harassed and defeated faces, those windy red-brick corridors with their clanging metal shutters, and the dead hand of suburbia over all. The bearded dominie who was the headmaster was, I believe, a kindly man and much loved, but to me he was an ogre and I still have a feeling of panic when I recall that awful voice, 'You boy. Come here.'[40]

Like Campbell, McNicol and McInnes, Moorehead found his senior days less frightening and more successful than his junior ones. His academic performance gradually improved so that he eventually matriculated, and he achieved a measure of sporting success as coxswain for the third rowing eight. He later made the University of Melbourne hockey team and even won a half-blue.[41]

McNicol, Campbell and McInnes all found at least one aspect of school life which they could excel at. Moorehead found none. He was, unlike McNicol, unimpressed with the masters, and unlike Campbell he lacked the quick wit to win respect from school fellows in social interaction or in extra-curricular activities such as debating. Sport was largely a closed book to him, while the church services were dull and dry, with 'hard seats, the arid and interminable sermons, the thin, flat singing of the hymns, the woe-begone and accusing images in cheap stained glass and mass-produced plaster – it was all one long punishment'. School life for Moorehead, because of his alienation from the dominant ideologies and ethos of the school, was a 'long incarceration . . . a memory I wish I could forget'.[42]

Others too, have written critical recollections of Scotch days. They are not considered in any depth here because the beauty of the memoirs of Glenn, McInnes, Campbell, McNicol and Moorhead is that they all refer to the same period of the school's existence, and use essentially the same form, thus enabling a comparison to be made of the differing recollections and experiences of the same school, in time as well as in name. But other recollections are worth mentioning to illustrate the fact that criticisms of Scotch have come from old boys and masters who have found the school barbaric, isolating and uninspiring, no matter the era in which they attended. In 1945 Arthur Davies, a former master at the school, published a satirical novel which portrayed ignorant and vicious boys under the charge of ill-informed and scarcely less vicious masters. One master refers to the boys approvingly: 'A decenter lot of kids you couldn't find. No brains of course, and rather a rough lot, but a thoroughly good crowd.'[43] Gladstone, a new teacher, realizes that the best way to keep his geography class happy is to not teach them geography, over the objections of 'a minority of narks who had a sordid, selfish desire to learn some. . . . They were totally lacking in school spirit',[44] while the approach to maintaining discipline is rough at best, one master advising: 'Kick 'em hard and they'll eat out of your hand. I once had a boy who stood up in class and called me a bastard. Just like that. I fetched him a crack on the jaw, and I've never had any trouble since. Not from him, anyway.'[45] The basic theme of Davies' satire is that lying, cheating and bluster will get both masters and boys further than a strict attention to the principles and official ideology of the school.

The most passionate denunciation of Scotch came, however, from Peter Blazey in his 1997 *Screw Loose: Uncalled-For Memoirs*. Later to become a political journalist, writer, gay liberation activist and press secretary for two ministers, Blazey, who died in 1997 of an AIDS-related illness, formed a passionate hatred for Scotch in his time as a pupil in the 1950s, a hatred which time did nothing to diminish:

> One of the finest functions a school can perform is to provide a person with a healthy object of hatred: few things can give a life more focus, and in this regard, Scotch College, Hawthorn, was perfect. In the fifties, it was philistine, militaristic and sports-obsessed; it was Calvinistic, male supremacist and even gerontophilic. . . . Scotch . . . was a repulsive exemplar of the Scottish 'cold shower' theory of education . . . run by a menagerie of teachers who were either tragic, neurotic failures or tough, reactionary bullies – all acting out the school's unlatinate code which seemed to be 'Kill or be Killed' . . . [most] would have failed basic personality testing, since many were Old Boys and virtually unemployable outside of this Hobbesian zoo.[46]

Blazey's description of this 'Caledonian hellhole' includes taunting a Jewish boy by calling him 'Cunty', being sexually molested by a priest, sexually molesting poddy-calves and the acquisition of sexual experience from school fellows, the last of which seems to have been the highlight of his schooldays.[47] It is as far from the school ideology as it is possible to get, and would have induced Littlejohn and other devoted ideologues of Christian manliness to turn in their graves if dead, and descend with greater haste into them if still alive.

Public schools in the nineteenth century became much more than simply academies of learning; they sought to become 'total' institutions that assumed control of a boy's academic progress, physical and sexual maturation and character development. Through rhetoric, symbols and manifest practice, they believed in the development of the 'whole man', partly through control of the boy's body, partly through control of his intellect, and significantly through control of his psychic outlook on the world. This mission remains, to some extent, to the present day; in the time of Glenn, McInnes, Campbell, McNicol and Moorehead it was explicitly outlined by the *Scotch Collegian*:

> From the very first day he should become imbued with the historical dignity which pervades his surroundings, and he feels that he is the heir to lofty traditions. . . . And so the idea of duty grows – the duty of playing a part in the life of the School until unconsciously, even if irresistibly, the immemorial spirit created by past generations stamps itself indelibly upon mind and soul, and with that spirit comes all that the School has held most dear of service and fair play.

It is a simple recipe: the school enunciates a value system and boys are inexorably drawn into supporting it.

Clearly, however, this was not the case. Alice Miller argued that one of the founding assumptions of how children should be raised in the West in the last 200 years has been that the child's will needs to be broken, a process often achieved through the violence of physical discipline.[48] Despite employing a range of more subtle methods alongside the infliction of corporal punishment, Scotch was only able to bend Glenn to its value system with any wholeheartedness. McInnes, Campbell and McNicol accepted only part of the ideology presented to them, while Moorehead appears to have rejected the lot.

The writings of this collection of 1920s old boys is evidence for the now well-understood sociological argument that all ideologies and social practices are bound up with practices of exclusion. Defining who is 'in' necessarily involves defining who is 'out'.[49] Toby Miller has suggested that the very categories used to exclude can also become rallying points for the excluded; but although McNicol and others may have found solace in the company of fellow 'swots', it is less clear that Moorehead was ever able to find such comfort.[50] Marginalized and excluded by the intolerable oppression of the reigning hegemony, boys such as

Moorehead suffered through miserable schoolboy years, the scars of which they bore for long after. Mangan, along with those whose contributions he built on and the contributions of those he inspired, has done much to illuminate the dominant or hegemonic educational ideologies in the public schools that played such important roles in the constituent colonies and countries of the British Empire and the Commonwealth in the nineteenth and twentieth centuries. The time has now come for a change of focus; through what means we can, through diaries, memoirs, letters and interviews, we should collectively turn our attention towards the lived experience of boys and men who learnt and operated in such environments. School history, sports history and the history of masculinity will be much advanced by such an endeavour.

NOTES

1. See also David Newsome, *Godliness and Good Learning: Four Studies on a Victorian Ideal* (London: John Murray, 1961) and Norman Vance, *The Sinews of the Spirit: The Ideal of Christian Manliness in Victorian Literature and Religious Thought* (Cambridge: Cambridge University Press, 1985).
2. J.A. Mangan, *Athleticism in the Victorian and Edwardian Public School: The Emergence and Consolidation of an Edwardian Ideology* (Cambridge: Cambridge University Press, 1981), pp.85–6.
3. J.A. Mangan, 'Introduction', in J.A. Mangan (ed.), *Pleasure, Profit, Proselytism: British Culture and Sport at Home and Abroad 1700–1914* (London: Frank Cass, 1988), p.2.
4. John Hargreaves, *Sport, Power and Culture: A Social and Historical Analysis of Popular Sports in Britain* (Cambridge: Polity Press, 1986), p.205.
5. Ibid., p.206.
6. For some exceptions dealing with how sport was used to spark local nationalism, see J.A. Mangan, 'Catalyst of Change: John Guthrie Kerr and the Adaptation of an Indigenous Scottish Tradition', in Mangan, *Pleasure, Profit, Proselytism*, pp.86–104, and Richard Cashman, 'Cricket and Colonialism: Colonial Hegemony and Indigenous Subversion?', in Mangan, *Pleasure, Profit, Proselytism*, pp.258–72.
7. See David W. Brown, 'Muscular Christianity in the Antipodes: Some Observations on the Diffusion and Emergence of a Victorian Ideal in Australian Social Theory', *Sporting Traditions*, 3 (1992), 173–87; Bob Stewart, 'Athleticism Revisited: Sport, Character Building and Protestant School Education in Nineteenth-Century Melbourne', *Sporting Traditions*, 9 (1992), 35–51; David Kirk, *Schooling Bodies: School Practice and Public Discourse 1880–1950* (London: Leicester University Press, 1998); Martin Crotty, 'Manly and Moral: The Making of Middle-Class Men in the Australian Public Schools', in J.A. Mangan and John Nauright (eds), *Sport in Australasian Society: Past and Present* (London and Portland, OR: Frank Cass, 2000), pp.11–30.
8. See Helen King, 'The Sexual Politics of Sport: an Australian Perspective', in Richard Cashman and Michael McKernan (eds), *Sport in History: The Making of Modern Sporting History* (Brisbane: University of Queensland Press, 1979), pp.68–85; Martin Crotty, *Making the Australian Male: Middle-Class Masculinity 1870–1920* (Melbourne, Melbourne University Press, 2001); R.W. Connell, *Masculinities* (Sydney: Allen and Unwin, 1995), p.77.
9. Crotty, *Making the Australian Male*, pp. 8, 41, 226.
10. Margot Fry, *Tom's Letters: The Private World of Thomas King, Victorian Gentleman* (Wellington: Victoria University Press, 2001).

11. See Crotty, *Making the Australian Male*, pp.221–33; James Mitchell, *A Deepening Roar: Scotch College, Melbourne, 1851–2001* (Sydney: Allen and Unwin, 2001).
12. Archie Glenn, *Things to be Remembered* (Melbourne: Diana Gribble, 1991), p.30.
13. Ibid., p.31.
14. Ibid., p.31.
15. Ibid., pp. 35–6.
16. Graham McInnes, *Goodbye Melbourne Town* (London: Hamish Hamilton, 1968), p.93.
17. Graham McInnes, *The Road to Gundagai* (London: Hamish Hamilton, 1968), p.104.
18. McInnes, *Goodbye Melbourne Town*, p.108.
19. McInnes, *The Road to Gundagai*, p.93.
20. Ibid., pp.92–3.
21. *Scotch Collegian*, 23 (1926), 9.
22. McInnes, *The Road to Gundagai*, pp.94–5.
23. Ibid., p.102; McInnes, *Goodbye Melbourne Town*, p.91.
24. Graham McInnes, *Humping My Bluey* (London: Hogarth Press, 1986), p.45.
25. Ibid., p.46.
26. Ross Campbell, *An Urge to Laugh* (Sydney: Wildcat Press, 1981), p.13.
27. Ibid., p.31.
28. Ibid., p.33.
29. Ibid., p.25.
30. Ibid., p.34.
31. David McNicol, *Luck's A Fortune: An Autobiography* (Melbourne: Sun Books, 1979), p.10.
32. Ibid., p.11.
33. Mangan, *Athleticism in the Victorian and Edwardian Public School*, esp. pp.135–8.
34. David W. Brown, 'Social Darwinism, Private Schooling and Sport in Victorian and Edwardian Canada', in Mangan, *Pleasure, Profit, Proselytism*, pp.221–2.
35. *Scotch Collegian*, 23 (1926), 210.
36. McNicol, *Luck's A Fortune*, p.13.
37. Ibid., p.12.
38. Ibid., pp.13, 16.
39. Alan Moorehead, *A Late Education: Episodes in a Life* (Melbourne: Penguin, 1976), p.20.
40. Ibid., pp.20–1.
41. Ibid., pp.25, 34.
42. Ibid., p.22.
43. Arthur Davies, *The Fiddlers of Drummond* (Sydney: Consolidated Press, 1945), p.52.
44. Ibid., p.78.
45. Ibid., p.91.
46. Peter Blazey, *Screw Loose: Uncalled-For Memoirs* (Sydney: Picador, 1997), pp.29–31.
47. Ibid., *passim*.
48. Alice Miller, *For Your Own Good: Hidden Cruelty in Child-Rearing and the Roots of Violence* (New York: Farrar, Strauss and Giroux, 1983), *passim*.
49. See, for example, Eve Kosofsky Sedgwick, *Epistemology of the Closet* (Baltimore, MD: Johns Hopkins University Press, 1990). See also Peter Stallybrass and Allon White, *The Politics and Poetics of Transgression* (Ithaca, NY: Cornell University Press, 1986), p.193.
50. Toby Miller, *The Well-Tempered Self: Citizenship, Culture and the Postmodern Subject* (Baltimore and London: The Johns Hopkins University Press, 1993), p.228.

7

Sport and Gender:
J.A. Mangan, Pioneer of Both
Projects and Publications

GIGLIOLA GORI

In 1996 I was approached by Professor J.A. ('Anthony') Mangan to write a chapter for a proposed volume on women emancipationists who, through their bodies and through sport, had defied convention, confronted prejudice, sought equality and achieved a considerable measure of success in these ambitions. The invitation was both attractive and well-timed. In Italy the walls of bias against women in sport still stood but the mortar was crumbling, the edifice was weakening and holes were appearing. Not only this but the voices of women academics in the fields of sports history and sport sociology were gradually being heard and their messages at least considered. Thus the timing of the request for involvement was cleverly opportune.

I appreciated that this was no accident. I was fully aware of, and had used for my own research and teaching an earlier equally well-timed volume aimed at the Anglo–Saxon world – somewhat ahead of the Mediterranean world with regard to studies of women and sport – J.A. Mangan's and Roberta J. Park's *From 'Fair Sex' to Feminism: Sport and the Socialization of Women in the Industrial and Post-Industrial Eras*, published in 1987. This pioneering work had also appeared at more or less the right moment (and is shortly to be reprinted). As was written in the Introduction to *From 'Fair Sex'*:

> While a considerable amount of work of feminist and social historians has been concerned with such topics as female complaints, sexual control, child birth, and health (topics which can be highly relevant for sports historians), little attention has been directed specifically to sport, recreation and leisure as a source of pleasure, an instrument of control or a symbol of emancipation. . . . [Consequently] it is hoped that this contribution

to social historical studies will stimulate inquiry into such issues and progressively deepen our understanding of the place of the women in the cultural heritage of modern society.[1]

Two comments are in order here. This quotation reveals Mangan's intellectual capacity to explore neglected themes requiring attention and his analytical ability to set modern sport in full cultural context.

I have to admit frankly that I was delighted with the eventually published collection, *Freeing the Female Body: Inspirational Icons* (2001). It dealt with notable women in their efforts to make their bodies their own, to be respected for endeavours in sport and admired for strength of body, mind and emotion in the most demanding competitive conditions. It was a ground-breaking contribution of quality to both women's studies and women's sports studies.

In terms of gender studies there was symmetry in the appearance of the volume. Mangan's earlier collections on masculinity and sport – in particular, as far as I am concerned, *Shaping the Superman: Fascist Body as Political Icon: Aryan Fascism* (1999), *Superman Supreme: Fascist Body as Political Icon: Global Fascism* (2000) and *Making European Masculinities: Sport, Europe, Gender* (2000) – had all been seminal contributions to gender studies in sport and now were being increasingly balanced by his gender publications involving women. Perhaps I will be forgiven for mentioning that he will publish my monograph *Female Bodies, Sport and Italian Fascism* in his very successful series 'Sport in the Global Society' – hence my special interest in the above volumes.

As early as 1987, of course, with the distinguished cultural historian James Walvin, Mangan had published a collection, *Manliness and Morality: Middle Class Masculinity in Britain and America 1850–1940*, which had been acclaimed for its originality of perspective.

In *Shaping the Superman*, Mangan himself contributed five out of the 11 chapters. One distinguished commentator praised him for considering so fruitfully a too-often ignored aspect of fascist culture with significant relevance for contemporary gender studies.[2] In a wider setting he was praised by another commentator as possibly an innovatory academic in sports studies who had brought together social anthropology, sociology and social history in a lucidly coherent and insightful analytical combination.[3]

In *Superman Supreme*, Mangan again illustrated his innovatory originality by publishing a collection (again with chapters by himself) on the global cult of the fascist male body. Then in *Making European Masculinities*, which contained two co-authored chapters involving the editor, he dealt with the unbroken thread, woven into the efforts of European societies in history, to ensure 'the fitness of the male – physical, moral, social and political – for confrontations with enemies, temptations and circumstances',[4] in a carefully organized 'atmosphere of aggressive competition, personal assertion and inculcated self-sacrifice'.[5]

Once again in this collection, Mangan displayed his scrupulous concern for human complexity. While he wrote in the Prologue that 'underlying much cultural reflection, planning and implementation associated with making men out of boys, has been training, both direct and indirect, for readiness for battlefields, on playing or similar venues',[6] he adds typically that this is not to deny 'the complexity of masculinity, the social or individual variations and the absence of a monolithic stereotype'.[7] He then reiterates that nevertheless in the face of a consortium of manly images and codes, 'the fundamental cultural image of the continually applauded male as aggressive, competitive, confrontational and dominant *when necessary* has been a constant phenomenon in the period under review in *Making European Masculinities*',[8] adding that 'while the twenty-first century is witnessing a gender revolution and change in history is not to be foolishly ignored [however] continuity in history is not to be naively overlooked'.[9]

It is timely here, apropos of such a remark, to mention how timely indeed Mangan's illuminating study of the male fascist body has been at the close of the twentieth century. In his Epilogue to *Shaping the Superman*, entitled simply 'Continuities', Mangan comments perceptively on the undercurrents of violence that are part and parcel of the daily life of Western societies, and directs our attention to a consequent range of muscular, mythical, contemporary media heroes, from Robocop to Rambo, who bring security through benign violence to an insecure world threatened by malign violence. Such figures, he points out, serve exactly the same purpose as the fascist massive musculatured supermen of Arnold Breker. They provide promise through strength and security born of superiority. If the 'images of Fascism', as Mangan notes, 'are bold, stark, direct and simple' and their message of 'success through strength; power through presentation; control through conviction'[10] unambiguous, the seductions of these elements are not overlooked by the manipulators of the modern media.

The media pages of Western newspapers are currently full of sagas of the superhero to be taken from the pages of comic books and transferred to the silver screen, including *Spider Man, Ghost Rider, Dare Devil*. The reason is clear: symbols of strength offer the fantasy of wish fulfilment – if not always the actuality – of indomitable security and immune safety.

Mangan's 'Continuities' points to another logical phenomenon of contemporary wish-fulfilment: the rise of the fighting superwomen – assertive, equal and self-empowered. He writes: 'Aggression is becoming part and parcel of sanctioned female gender image projection at the same time as physical aggression is rising among women. All this is logical: equality brings access, opportunity – and responsibility! Are we now to speak in one breath of the Warrior Superman and Superwomen?'[11] Thus, as he then states:

> today are to be found [modern] variants of the Aryan Superman – in democracies of course, always a defender, never an aggressor but a continuing and permanent iconographic presentation – an image, gender free, purified of its threats, dangers and immoralities, that powerfully engages the senses. The image is not of the Wild Man but Wonderman and Wonderwoman. The Malign Fascist Superman has been replaced by the Benign Superman and Superwoman of the Free World![12]

All this is impressive enough – the debt to J.A. Mangan on the part of historians, sociologists and others in sports studies has accumulated with these and other publications, and is substantial. However, in his Epilogue to *Freeing the Female Body*, he went beyond the role of seeker of those with important things to say as well as relevatory commentator on masculinity, sport and culture, and himself took on the role of someone with important things to say about women, sport, emancipation and the *future*. First, he reminded his readers that *Freeing the Female Body*

> has sought to discover . . . how some women in modern time, through a re-evaluation, reconstruction and rehabilitation of their bodies and women's bodies in general, have influences and determined, directly and indirectly and to a greater or lesser extent, the status of modern women of the modern 'global village'.[13]

He then pointed out quite correctly that what the selected women in *Freeing the Female Body* 'all demonstrated and to a degree determined through their determination, is that, despite historical belief, assertion and demand, women are not to be relegated primarily or predominantly to reproduction, nor to subscription to the uterine tradition that defines women's bodies according to their reproductive potential',[14] and that most properly, women 'increasingly render themselves, and are rendered by the commentator more visible in history'.[15]

Such nuanced and careful comments are in marked contrast, for example, to one group of recent male academics, who wrongly and simplistically have remarked that 'women can represent the nation in static iconographic forms, but as bodies in motion they will not do'.[16] The women in *Freeing the Female Body* give the lie not once but again and again to such naivety – a naivety made all the more obvious by the authors' offering of only two Australian incidences as 'evidence'! How globally representative is the notorious macho culture of Australia? Indeed how representative are two Australian incidents? Prejudice, ignorance and indifference towards women in sport still exist. This is recognized. However, things have changed and are changing for the better, as *Freeing the Female Body* demonstrates in some detail. Sweeping generalizations made for dramatic effect are quite simply poor scholarship, and academically unacceptable.

In his Epilogue to *Freeing the Female Body* Mangan then goes on to make two points of significance for future research into women and sport: that successful women have been mostly middle–class, and that the support of their families 'made them' in the sense that it provided crucial domestic, financial and emotional sustenance through often hard struggles. What of the present with its state endorsement, regional encouragement, school support and increasing equality of opportunity? Do these factors cut across class advantage and negate past class assets?

Perhaps the most significant comments by Mangan in this Epilogue involve his request for complexity of perception in analysing women in society. This has clear implications for women in sport. He warns against polemical simplicity with its inflexible stereotyping of women too sweepingly as victims and men as merely monstrous 'monolithic' supporting players. Such simplistic subscription to 'victimization' demeans women. He suggest that there is a failure in too many studies of women in society, culture and sport 'to fully assess women's actual power, covert and overt, in male and female relationships whatever the *ostensible* formal, institutional, cultural and political framework'.[17]

This is a challenging assertion and his request for complexity of analysis is equally challenging. What he is saying surely is that it is time to move beyond oppression, victimization, injustice and prejudice – while never overlooking their existence (why else would he be so concerned to prove their existence and to demonstrate how some women have marvellously overcome them?) and seek the complexity of reality.

There is an academic integrity at work here. Accurate analysis, not polemical point-scoring, is the bedrock foundation of the academic edifice. These challenges are to be respected and given serious consideration. They will ensure better informed, more careful, more complete studies of women in sport in the future as women gain more control, influence and power.

In his helpfully provocative Epilogue Mangan suggests other matters to which analysts should give their attention: closer consideration of the relationship between women and women in the struggle for female emancipation through sport, and therefore consideration of the female conservatives and reactionaries who restricted rather than advanced the movement. Elsewhere he suggests an intelligent awareness that the struggle for freedom is not 'an inexorable linear progression' towards advantageous liberty. It carries penalties as well as privileges, and wrongs as well as rights – *women*-induced. He points out in other writings to the increasing and worrying statistics on women and smoking and drinking and the rise of female heart disease and alcoholism. Not all problems are male-induced! There is also the fact that there may be ever-increasing numbers of female sports stars but too many adolescent girls play too little sport, despite the opportunities now available. If a lack of freedom brings denial, freedom brings the choice to deny.

Enough has almost been written above to indicate the nature of J.A. Mangan's constructive reflections on women, emancipation, sport and future enquiries. Two quotations from his Epilogue to *Freeing the Female Body* will complete my commentary:

> In the past, while to an extent (but to what extent?) men determined the identity of women, dictated what is desirable, demanded what was acceptable and denied what was unacceptable, in that concrete world of men and women as distinct from the abstract world of political publication, women also made their own demands of other women – and of men. These realities receive far

less attention from feminism but they are crucial to a subtle analysis of the power relations between women and men and women and women.[18]

and

> What is required in studies of women (and men) and their bodies is a recognition of what is universal and what is particular at a number of levels, for the simple reason that concepts of the body are considerably culturally determined and individually interpreted and there are many cultures and many layers within cultures and numerous individual men and women. *Any* 'essentialism' is to be avoided – including a feminist 'essentialism' of masculinity.[19]

Finally, towards the end of the Epilogue, Mangan calls for a sophisticated 'pluralism in analysis dealing in cultural differences and similarities, a recognition of both willing and unwilling accommodation, adaptation and compliance', the embracing of 'cultural, class and racial "specificities", both historical and contemporary',[20] as well as a more thorough analysis of women's power through the body – for instance, in the realm of sexuality: how it is enhanced, how it is maintained and how it is retained, and the consequences of the pressures on women – and concludes that 'it will then be increasingly clear that tendencies to dichotomous analysis of power and powerlessness in the past and present increasingly will be found wanting'.[21]

There is much to 'chew over' in this Epilogue. It illustrates J.A. Mangan's continual search for balance in perspective, rigour in analysis and accuracy in conclusion. We all in sports studies owe him much.

NOTES

1. 'Introduction', in J.A. Mangan and Roberta J. Park (eds), *From 'Fair Sex' to Feminism: Sport and the Socialization of Women in the Industrial and Post-industrial Eras* (London: Frank Cass, 1987), pp.2–3 and 9.
2. Jeffrey Richards, review of J.A. Mangan, *Shaping the Superman: Fascist Body as Political Icon: Aryan Fascism* (London and Portland, OR: Frank Cass, 1999), *Culture, Sport, Society*, 3, 1 (Spring, 2000), 89. Richards wrote that *Superman* was 'an authoritative, thought-provoking and readable discussion of an aspect of Fascist ideology which has received comparatively little serious attention to date'.
3. See the review by Richard Hill of E.G. Dunning *et al.*, *The Sports Process* (Champaign, IL: Human Kinetics, 1993) in *The International Journal of the History of Sport*, 17, 4 (Dec. 2000), 211.
4. J.A. Mangan, 'Prologue: With Spirits Masculine', in J.A. Mangan (ed.), *Making European*

Masculinities: Sport, Europe, Gender (*The European Sports History Review*, 2) (London and Portland, OR: Frank Cass, 2000), p.1.

5. Ibid.
6. Ibid., p.3.
7. Ibid., p.2.
8. Ibid.
9. Ibid., p.3.
10. J.A. Mangan, 'Icon of Monumental Brutality: Art and the Aryan Man', in J.A. Mangan (ed.), *Shaping the Superman: Fascist Body as Political Icon: Aryan Fascism* (London and Portland, OR: Frank Cass, 2000), p.131.
11. J.A. Mangan, 'Epilogue: Continuities', in *Shaping the Superman*, p.186.
12. Ibid., pp.103–4.
13. J.A. Mangan and Fan Hong (eds), *Freeing the Female Body: Inspirational Icons* (London and Portland, OR: Frank Cass, 2001), p.237.
14. Ibid.
15. Ibid., p. 238.
16. Toby Miller *et al.*, *Globalization and Sport: Playing the World* (London: Sage, 2001), pp.2–3.
17. Mangan and Hong, *Freeing the Female Body*, p.239.
18. Ibid., p.245.
19. Ibid., p.246.
20. Ibid., p.248.
21. Ibid.

Sport, Society and Militarism – In Pursuit of the Democratic Soldier: J.A. Mangan's Exploration of Militarism

VASSIL GIRGINOV

SOCIETY, MILITARISM AND SPORT: AN INTRODUCTION

On entry visitors to the history of the Holocaust section at the Museum of Tolerance in Los Angeles are given a photo passport of a child. Throughout the tour of the museum the passport is updated and the ultimate fate of the particular child is revealed. James Anthony Mangan's explorations of militarism are of a similar nature to this photo passport. He systematically unveils the sociopolitical background of militarism and interrogates its relations with sport in the socialization of boys, not only in his native Britain but also across the globe. The principal difference between these two explorations is that, while the Holocaust, the ultimate example of man's inhumanity to man, is virtually a closed chapter, Mangan's explorations of militarism continue. Writing in 1990 about the attempts of British imperialism to influence the minds and emotions of its captive audience, Mangan stated that *Making Imperial Mentalities* revealed 'how much remains to be done before the *full process and its consequences for the imperial and post-imperial world* are documented and analysed'.[1] His latest collaborative work on sport as a substitute for war[2] and on masculinity, field sports, hunting and militarism[3] are yet other valuable contributions in exploring these pathways.

Mangan published his first analysis on sport and militarism in the 1970s and has remained engaged with the topic ever since. Such consistent effort represents a remarkable programme of research spanning more than a quarter of a century, resulting in dozens of books, editorials, articles, conference papers and dissertations, often in collaboration with scholars from all continents. To offer a critique of work of such a magnitude would be, without a doubt, a daunting task.

Moreover, as Mangan himself fully appreciates in his *Athleticism*, which has become accepted as a classic work, 'any analytical scheme is partial'.[4] This paper, therefore, attempts something rather more achievable.

The title of this contribution, as the reader will have noticed, suggests an obvious contradiction captured by the notion of the 'democratic soldier'. Borrowing from James Toner's 'magnificent anomaly'[5] helps in a succinct way to establish the backdrop against which, in what follows, the ethics of sport as an element of an emerging progressive and democratic civil order are examined in relation to militarism which, to use Samuel Huntington's words, 'emphasizes the permanence, irrationality, weakness and evil in human nature'.[6] No critique of an academic work is immune from the risk of simplifying, misinterpreting or missing out on a perspective. As he whose legacy is being scrutinized put it, 'any blindness of vision is yours'. This contribution, therefore, ventures to address this problem by setting from the beginning, a framework for a critical reading of Mangan. It revolves around two interrelated rubrics: (i) the meaning of militarism, its main constituent and relationship to Mangan's interpretation of sport, and (ii) an analytical map guiding the critical examination which consists of an approach to history – historicism and three recurring themes, of ideology, power and narratives (seen also as a structuralist technique) – devised from a broad reading of Mangan's work.

THE PROJECT OF MILITARISM: NATIONAL AND GLOBAL DIMENSIONS AND INTERPRETATIONS

The study of militarism presents serious theoretical and methodological problems. Consequently, attempts to examine its relations to wider social processes such as education, socialization or the formation of mentalities inevitably encounter similar problems. This is partly because writers of all schools of thought have attempted to relate intellectual ideas, political strategies, rhetoric and class struggles to studies of militarism. The problem is compounded further by the fact that debates on the subject have tended to shift their focus in line with changing social, political and economic realities before and after world and regional wars.

There is no consensus among students of this problem as to what exactly militarism is and how it originated. According to the German historian Werner Conze, the term 'militarism' first appeared in the *Memoirs* of Madame de Chastenay in 1816/18.[7] Hans Herzfeld, a foremost authority in this field, argued that a debate about militarism originated in England in relation to the formation of the modern state.[8] Whatever the truth about the origin of militarism, in either case the main concern was about the relationship between the civil and military element in society.

A broad review of various attempts to theorize militarism suggests that writers in the Marxist and the liberal traditions put forward different elements. Michael Klare defined militarism as the tendency of

> a nation's *military apparatus* (which includes the armed forces and associated paramilitary, intelligence and bureaucratic agencies) to assume *ever-increasing control* over the lives and behaviour of its citizens; the *military goals* (preparation for war, acquisition of weaponry, development of military industries), and *military values* (centralization of authority, hierarchization, discipline and conformity, combativeness and xenophobia).[9]

Since the debate about militarism and the military contest itself have occupied a large part of German and British sociology and political theory, it is instructive for an analysis to identify both their similarities and differences. Among the many German writers in this area, the influential work of Karl Kautsky offered some useful insights, as he and Jesuit Pachtler were the first who suggested that militarism should be studied in the context of capitalist development and that it was consonant with capitalism. Kautsky identified three main elements of militarism: the system of military discipline; its extension to the state and civil society; and the military sector of the economy. One of his followers, Rosa Luxemburg, developed further this concept and proposed that militarism was an important 'province of accumulation' in the sense that capital employs militarism for implementing a foreign and colonial policy.[10] However, as Stargardt pointed out, German 'militarism not only represented the perennial threat of coercion: it was also built on consent, thereby enmeshing both the state and society in an all-encompassing system of power'.[11]

This observation on the nature of German militarism helps to distinguish between three crucial elements. First, it suggests that the building of the modern Western state and its power should be seen in conjunction with the development of its military power; second, it is useful to distinguish between the state institutions that secure obedience (e.g, the army, police, law courts) and those that manufacture consent, such as schools, the church and the media; and third, the military power of the German state which was established on the basis of mass support.

Few examples could better aid our understanding of the differences between German and British militarism than the opening episode in Nicholas Stargardt's book on 'The German Idea of Militarism'. In this true story, a 57-year-old shoemaker and ex-convict who wanted a passport to leave Germany embarked on a strange mission. On the strength of wearing the military uniform of a captain of the German army, he commanded two squads of soldiers to follow him on the train from Berlin to the town of Kopenick, where, with the cooperation of senior figures, he usurped the municipal administration, arrested the mayor and seized 2,000,000 marks from their coffers. While this episode caused a furore in Germany, in Britain, *The Times* 'remarked archly that such things were only possible in Germany'.[12] As Stargardt concluded, the uniform made the man.

The British idea of militarism, despite some common elements with the German (and French), as Mangan is at pains to stress, is based on a different set of social, political and economic concerns. Its formal inception can be attributed to the 1689 Bill of Rights, which sought to lay down the principles of modern liberalism and democracy. An essential element of the formation of the new state was the relationship between the civilian government and the military. The importance of the problem for contemporaries is evidenced by the titles of two books published in 1697: John Trenchard's *An Argument Showing That a Standing Army is Inconsistent With a Free Government and Absolutely Distructive To The Constitution of the English Monarchy* and Andrew Fletcher's *A Discourse Concerning Militias and Standing Armies With Relation to the Past and Present Governments of Europe and of England in Particular.*[13]

At a philosophical level, discussions reflect the fundamental debate about liberal individualism and social organization of the state as proposed by Herbert Spencer[14] in his pioneering work on the industrial and the militant type of societies in the mid-1880s. Similar developments in economic writings, and in particular John Hobson's 1902 study *Imperialism* and Norman Angell's 1910 book *The Great Illusion: A Study of the Relation of Military Power in Nations to their Economic and Social Advantage* provided influential (though rather naive) arguments about the inherently peaceful nature of capitalist industrialization, warned about the dangers of wars for all parties involved, and promoted concepts of international finance, industry and free trade.

From a geopolitical and military point of view, England also followed a different road. The politics of militarism, despite popular rhetoric for improving 'national efficiency' never favoured the military over the civil interests in society. In 1912, when France appointed General Joseph Joffre to the newly created supreme military post of Chef d'état-major-general and increased the period of military service from two to three years, his British counterpart, Field-Marshal Lord Roberts, had to resign in order to promote the proposal for a system of national service. The reality of mass conscription was received with hostility, and no more than 2.7 per cent of the male population aged between 15 and 49 were members of the Volunteer Force.[15]

In contrast to continental Europe, where armies were becoming gradually a key constituent of an emerging centralized state, Britain's geographical location as an island did not require maintaining a large standing army; only a navy. This, however, allowed the traditional role of the army to be extended into what became known as 'naval militarism' and 'colonial militarism'. Britain established itself as a dominant and aggressive naval power capable of securing empire and influence in Europe – which in 1500 included some 500 political units, reduced by 1900 to 25. The chief mechanism for this natural selection was military competition. The achievement of hegemony, as Alex Callinicos commented, 'was underpinned by a rising level of military expenditure: the real spending of the British state rose fifteenfold between 1700 and 1815 with civil expenses never rising above 23 percent of total outlay'.[16] Britain also won the race with Germany, where military spending at the end of the nineteenth century amounted to about 90 per cent of the Reich budget. In the words of Charles Tilly, 'the preparation for war has been the great state-building activity'.[17] This was achieved, among other things, as result of a cross-party consensus and a very progressive and flexible centralized income-tax system that at the same time allowed investments to be made in social programmes such as mass education. One could not safely subscribe, however, to the popular belief that because historical circumstances shaped the British army to be simultaneously political, professional and aristocratic, it has always been apolitical. Hew Strachan's *The Politics of the British Army*[18] clearly demonstrates that, throughout history, the officer corps has flexed systematically its political muscles. The relationship between military expertise and political control has been a changing one, marked by a steady growth of centralized civilian control over the military, as Paul Smith's study on *Government and Armed Forces in Britain 1856–1990*[19] has documented.

Alfred Vagts's seminal study of militarism captured neatly different understandings and interpretations of militarism. Two in particular of his conclusions are worth noting. First, he saw militarism as a tendency to extend dominion, and thus as akin to imperialism. Second, Vagts attempted to link continental Europe's idea of militarism, revolving around a state of mind, with the Anglo–Saxon concern for civilian control,[20] thus advancing a wider view beyond the boundaries of local or regional definitions. Nevertheless, as Stargardt argued persuasively, 'militarism is a term of critical appraisal. It never was nor could be an objective category of analysis, except by lopping off all its wider meanings in order to make it synonymous with a single issue, like the arms race.' He continued the argument by proposing that 'because militarism is a rhetorical rather than a rigorous theoretical concept, it is intimately connected to the intentions, programmes, strategies and propaganda of political actors'.[21]

Volker Berghahn's review of the history of the international debate on militarism (from 1861 to 1979)[22] echoed this conclusion and suggested that various states promote different understandings of this concept. For the Americans, the term is defined as policy, preparedness, exalting military virtues and relying on force in international relations; the French see it as a political system based upon the army; the Italians emphasize the prevalence of a military spirit in a state; the Spanish are similarly concerned with the predominance of the military element in government; the former Soviets talk about a closed system of economics, politics and ideology; the Germans view the predominance of military forms as thought patterns and objectives in state, politics and society; whereas the British appear to favour the spirit of the professional soldier, the prevalence of military sentiment among a people and the tendency to regard military efficiency as paramount interest of the state.

In summation, this discussion on the origins and interpretations of the project of militarism has suggested that:

- it is a complex social, political and economic phenomenon that is closely related to the building of the modern Western state, and the British state in particular; or to use Marek Thee's words, militarism's 'foremost breeding ground is to be found in state formation and the military profession'.[23] However, as Mangan reminds us in his studies of imperialism and fascism, a fertile breeding ground can be the education system – public *and* private;

- it is a product of the complex interplay between national developments (as state of mind, culture and perception) and global developments (of imperialism, conquest for territories and influence). This entails that studies on militarism ought to account equally for national and international perceptions of it. In this regard, Mangan's work supplies useful examples;

- it involves political actors (state and government institutions) and non-political actors (voluntary organizations and individuals);

- it is a hegemonic project which requires mass support (in the form of obedience or consent), and the promotion of powerful ideologies, strategies and practical policies on the part of those in power as well as struggles with those opposing it;

- it involves two broad levels of analysis – of social and economic structures (also referred to as 'militarization') and of cultural superstructures (or 'militarism' in the form of patterns of values, ideologies, norms and symbols and associated institutions); and

- any engagement with militarism that concentrates only on the use of military ethics and practices, including sport, for preparing youth for discipline and war would be one-sided. Equal attention has to be paid to what has been done for the preservation of liberal freedoms and democracy. In this respect, Mangan has made shrewd observations on the use of militaristic images in the preservation of democracy in the epilogue of his *Shaping the Superman*.[24]

As this contribution demonstrates, Mangan's analysis draws equally on the notions of the professional soldier; it adds to the fundamental historical debate about universal conscription and the role of the army in British society; the military sentiment, or the 'spectacular theatre' as MacKenzie[25] has eloquently described the press representations of nineteenth-century British imperialism as entertaining, heroic adventures in distant colonies; and the military efficiency that underpinned most Victorian and Edwardian public physical education and sport policies, aimed at preparing the future leaders of the Empire in martial and 'non-martial' roles. What is an original contribution in his analysis is the fusion of three analytical perspectives, of social anthropology, sociology and social history, for a deeper understanding of militarism and its role in shaping modern sport.

One of Mangan's foremost analytical virtues has been to define militarism quite specifically and to show how in the era of British neo-imperialism, in terms of this definition, middle-class youths in private (public) schools were prepared on playing fields for battlefields. His has been an important revisionist perspective, which rebuts simplistic arguments about non-militaristic imperial society. Such arguments overlook major British sources and are myopically preoccupied with the lack of conscription, large standing armies or state support. In a range of publications he has demonstrated the validity of this perspective.

A further analytical virtue is his argument that all nations – democratic and totalitarian – promote images of the warrior hero (consider the mass of contemporary material on the SAS) to a lesser or greater extent, in the interest of survival. In his recent studies of fascism he has drawn attention to the problem of benign warrior images – both men and women (as is appropriate in an age of gender equality, female assertion and new female aggression) in Western nations, especially the United States, as mechanisms for the preservation and sustenance of liberal freedoms and democracy itself. In the forthcoming volume *Militarism, Sport, Europe,* he will examine idealism propelling sport as an alleged instrument of substitution for, and antidote to, and a replacement for war.[26]

'ALL NATIONS NEED SOLDIERS AT SOME TIME
OR OTHER TO SURVIVE AND TO THRIVE':
ENGAGING MILITARISM WITH SPORT

Since the purpose of the last section was to set the scene for a critical examination of the relationship between civil and military elements in Mangan's work, an important clarification should be made at this point. Mangan never ventured to study militarism per se. Initially, he came to a study of militarism, among other matters, by way of his interest in the socialization of the young. His main concern was threefold. First, research into the world-famous English public schools convinced him that late Victorian education constituted in part an introduction into imperial militarism. Second, he was struck by the poorly researched and inaccurate generalizations of the sports historian Richard Holt, based on an inadequate reading and understanding of these schools and his narrow predilection for working-class activities.[27] Third, and most important, Mangan always has been concerned with socialization into society and the role of sport in this process. Those, like the author, who suspected there was somehow a strong link between Mangan's personal history and significant others and his concern with imperial militarism, would be disappointed to realize that his academic endeavours were not inspired by family traditions or instilled by his father's heroic bedtime stories (he was wounded in the First World War). There were none. His interest was, and is, how do cultures socialize the young into their belief systems. He came to the very reassuring conclusion that sport was a major means in many of them.

In this interest, the soldier in empire and his extraordinary success has intrigued Mangan. As he put it in a personal communication,

> for practical soldiering success the hard lessons of the public schools seemed pertinent, appropriate and successful. All nations need soldiers at some time or other to survive and to thrive – hence my interest in how they are successfully 'made' and how boys (and girls now) will always be conditioned into aggression for society's benefit.[28]

However, he has also shown how a public-school training was equally pertinent to the success of imperial administrators. The rest of this section uses the main approach of historicism and the three recurring themes identified in the introduction – of ideology, power and narratives – to map the work of Mangan on sport and militarism.

Historicism

Mangan's approach to history is not bound to a single theoretical perspective; rather, as he defines it, it is 'intensive-comparative'. What this analytical pairing entails is a critical historicism which constructs histories through an interpretive process and not simply by recording 'facts'. 'The first tenet of historicism,' observed Lee Harvey, 'is that history is an interpretive process.'[29] Similarly, Alun Munslow argued in his review of E.H. Carr's *What is History?*, arguably the most influential book in the historiographical revolution in Britain,

> my history is historicism in that I want to see history as a contemporary and emancipatory cultural practice, and I do not think a narrow concentration on finding out the empirical reality is the only thing required in order to do that – you can use moral argument and non-empiricist positions just as well to know something about the past.[30]

These views are shared by Mangan, who questioned Robert Merton's categorization of species of academic investigators: the European preoccupied with interaction that should logically occur, and the American concerned with relations that empirically exist,[31] by suggesting that a third category, combining the two, is also possible and equally fruitful for understanding reality. The outcome of this type of investigation is a critical approach to history which, to use Harvey's description again, 'locates events in their social and political context, addresses the economic constraints and engages taken-for-granted ideological factors'.[32] This is an approach that is consistent with conclusions made in the previous section.

Mangan's use of this interpretive, critical and objective historicism to reconstruct the meaning of events is best illustrated in his *Athleticism in the Victorian and Edwardian Public School*, praised as a 'classic' by two most distinguished cultural historians. Here, rather than taking for granted social structures such as education or athleticism (which was generally perceived as an anti-intellectual pursuit) to inform a current history, he deconstructed these social structures and employed them as the basis for historical analysis. This approach involves a carefully designed method for uncovering the historical evidence, typically based on case studies. The meaning of the evidence, however, depends upon a simultaneous reconceptualization of the same dominant social structures.

The interplay between construction and deconstruction of abstract theoretical notions – for example, the reproduction of social class and its ideology – is facilitated by the use of critical case studies to identify social practices and to explore how they operate in the social totality. For Mangan, these social practices are responsible for establishing a 'process of circular causality'. In other words, perpetuating the values and practices of athleticism through a rigidly organized educational process aimed at creating generations of well-imbued citizens of the empire, who are then employed in key positions in the same educational system that produced them. The 'total universe' becomes the British public-school system and middle- and upper-class society. Ideology, power and narratives constitute an essential part of this process.

Ideology

The notion of ideology is central in Mangan's work. It underpins all the key processes to which sport contributes: those of asserting national identity, making imperialist mentalities, justifying policies and shaping sports practices. He charged athleticism with the responsibility of being an educational ideology and investigated the means by which it is created and sustained. In doing that he assumed that learning and teaching have social implications that exceed the mere measurement of knowledge and skills acquisition. Equally, he depicted schooling as an institution in which philosophy, structure and practices are continually related to wider issues of social production and reproduction. This, however, is achieved in a controversial way. We accept that schools promote social science knowledge, which is inevitably about the past, but their mission is to prepare future citizens. When the Victorian and Edwardian schools set out to employ sport to cultivate desirable moral values, physical and moral courage, loyalty and cooperation, the capacity to act fairly and to take defeat well, and the ability to command and obey, they were effectively engaged in projecting and actively shaping the lives of youth. An undertaking of this kind is inherently cultural, political and ideological. As Thomas Popkewitz commented, 'when we adopt a belief that knowledge is about prediction and administration, we have left science and its relation to the empirical world to move into the realm of ideology and social control'.[33]

Mangan, quite rightly, does not dwell laboriously on the meaning and interpretations of ideology. Again, he demonstrates an attractive balance. He accepts that athleticism was a public-school ideology that 'embraced a complex of ideas and feelings deliberately and carefully created through ritual and symbol; that it was, on occasion, a form of "pseudo-reasoning", a deliberate rationalization for ambitions such as status and power; and that it constituted value-judgements masquerading as facts to reinforce commitment'.[34] At the same time he recognized that 'the ideology involved virtuousness, indulgence and expedience; it embraced idealism, casuistry and opportunism. It was, in fact, a complex manifestation.'[35]

As an ideology, athleticism performs a dual role for the public schools – to prepare 'captains of industry' and 'leaders of empire'. Recently Mangan has extended his inquiries (with Colm Hickey) into the elementary school and the existence of 'adapted athleticism' with the purpose of elementary schools 'teaching the poor how to play' through socially controlled activities – hence, as in the case of public schools, bringing ideology and practice together. The dialectic between social needs, practice, ideas and ideology is captured by the notion of hegemony. Mangan treats hegemony as 'the power to shape consciousness and, within education . . . the power to define what is valued knowledge'.[36] From a critical perspective, he has been concerned with ways in which social, cultural and economic conditions produce certain selectivity in the process of promoting physical education and sport. The working definitions of ideology and hegemony serve the analysis well. Initially they have purposefully concentrated mostly on the role of the middle-class male and left other classes, women and state activities, for others to investigate. Sport and socialization is a large area as mentioned above.

Nevertheless in recent writings Mangan has turned his attention to elementary schools and the role of sport within them and in two edited volumes, with Roberta Park and Fan Hong respectively, he has produced two well-received volumes on women, sport and socialization. After all, only so much can be done in one academic lifetime. 'Teaching the poor how to play' was not originally part of athleticism, and Mangan and Hickey contend that 'athleticism (of elementary schools) was not the athleticism of the public and grammar schools'.[37] However, as its influence grew, it started to spread beyond the boundaries of the 'process of circular causality' and involved concerns about recreation and sport for the middle and working classes. This is precisely the role of ideology – to mobilize mass support by producing a technical or instrumental rationality needed to sustain a particular social order. British imperialism of the late nineteenth and early twentieth century was a hegemonic project that sought to establish elements of a new accumulation regime (or what Rosa Luxemburg called 'militarism as a province of accumulation'), in large part by establishing a new approach to social and political regulation, but one that did not envisage the militarization of public life. Hegemony, as Bob Jessop argued persuasively 'involves the interpellation and organization of different "class-relevant" (but not necessarily class-conscious) forces under the "political, intellectual and moral leadership" of . . . its political, intellectual and moral spokesmen. The key to exercise of such leadership is the development of a specific "hegemonic project".'[38]

Here, 'interpellation' is described as the ideological mechanism through which subjects are endowed with specific identities, social positions and interests. This mechanism in turn is grounded in the accumulation of cognitive and organizational learning capacities developed through agents' interactions. Athleticism, as part of the wider process of political socialization, has been used for interpellation in the contest for hegemony and leadership. In that sense it bears resemblance with the pre-capitalist strategies for political accumulation and state-building found in the practices of English lords. In an attempt to increase their income, the lords decided to redistribute 'wealth and income away from their peasants or from other members of the exploiting class. This meant they had to deploy their resources towards building up their *means of coercion* – by investment in military men and equipment.'[39] The growing democratization of society entailed that in order to preserve its main ideological function and the status of those who promoted it, athleticism had to spread its gospel beyond the public schools. Athleticism, therefore, is more than an ideology. It is an essential element of the process of political accumulation which forms a bridge between its two constituents – warfare and state-building. Mangan has highlighted this *dual* role of athleticism in his observation of its 'pure' form as found in public schools (based on facilities and free time) between 1850 and 1870.

But if athleticism was the educational ideology of the dominant class in Britain, it would be instructive to acknowledge its contribution to the systematic distortion of interaction and language as well in the form of structural (power) relations, policies and public discourse. We turn to these matters later.

Hegemony, in Gramsci's terms, relates to the struggle to provide moral and political leadership, but he also allowed for the development of alliances beyond solely class-based groupings. The outcome of these struggles is always uncertain, and as Ian Henry commented, in relation to the paternalistic role of the middle and upper classes to exercise social control over leisure policy in the late nineteenth century, 'such reading of history fails to acknowledge the fact that working-class groups successfully resisted certain forms of paternalism, while selectively accepting others'.[40] Moreover, as Popkewitz reminded us, 'the determination of futures is not reserved for particular elites and experts who claim a sacred knowledge'.[41]

The British state became very active in intervening across a range of social, political and economic activities. Several public health acts were introduced (in 1848, 1872, 1875 and in the 1866 Sanitation Act) and also Forster's 1870 Education Act. Cross-class alliances for promoting sport and recreation were also commonplace. In 1886 a group of outstanding politicians, educators and sportspersons established the National

Physical Recreation Society with Herbert Gladstone, MP, son of the British Prime Minister W.E. Gladstone, as president. The purpose of the society was to promote physical recreation among the working classes. Similarly, a silver medallist in the 1863 Liverpool Olympic Festival, Lord William Lennox, in his essay on physical education, praised the Wenlock Olympian Society as a great idea. Despite its being out of the reach of the great centres of learning, arts, politics and fashion, he wrote of it:

> The benefits indeed are obvious. It improves the mind, strengthens the body, invigorates the race . . . and so keeps men out of beer-shops . . . and drags them out into the fresh clean air of heaven to get health and fun together. . . . Now I call this a thoroughly English society, and Wenlock must be proud of it.[42]

Another influential figure, A.J. Balfour, an Eton and Cambridge disciple, and Prime Minister from 1902 to 1908, in 1905 helped in the House of Commons to found the British Olympic Association. More importantly still, he was responsible for the Education Act of 1902 which, according to Peter McIntosh, 'did not specifically reform physical education, but the same ideas which prompted the Act also profoundly influenced the theory and practice of physical education, and the Act itself did produce the administrative framework without which the subsequent rapid developments of physical education would hardly have been possible'.[43]

Without specific reference to the Balfour Act but with appropriate emphasis on the earlier crucial influence of the cross-transmission which transformed the teacher training colleges and thus the elementary schools, and so led directly to the 1902 Act and more importantly the recommendations of 1906, Mangan and Colm Hickey discuss at length the implications of some of these ideas. They state that 'after 1906 the introduction of athleticism into the elementary schools was state pedagogical policy and this policy was in the hands of public school educated state officials'.[44]

From an ideological point of view, it is important to note that at the end of the nineteenth century sport was also ascribed the role of an antidote to war and militarism. In 1891 at the International Peace Congress in Rome, a well-known English pacifist, Hodson Pratt, called for annual international sport and poetry festivals for students (today's World Student Games in embryo) in the pursuit of international amity. It is no coincidence that Pierre de Coubertin included five winners of the Nobel Peace Prize among the honorary members of the International Olympic Committee when he founded it in 1894. Of course, not all members of the British upper class subscribed to that view. Even Lord Balfour, despite his involvement in sport, remained jaundiced about the role of sport in promoting peace. When in 1920 Philip Noel-Baker (later to be awarded the Nobel Peace Prize) told him he was leaving a meeting early to go to Antwerp to take part in the Olympic Games, Balfour exclaimed in horror: 'You are going to the Olympics? To stir up quarrels and rivalries and hatred among the nations?'[45]

Enough in the space available has been said about the role of sport in promoting military attitudes and skills, but as yet relatively little analysis is available revealing its contribution in opposing the same military education and in promoting peace. Hence, as stated earlier, the importance of *Militarism, Sport, Europe: War without Weapons*. To define a particular phenomenon, some commentators employ a well-rehearsed analytical tool based on the notion of what that phenomenon is not. Mangan is well aware of the benefits offered by this approach in understanding the relationship between militarism and civil society when he refers to Roger Griffin's proposition that the dynamics of fascism can be best understood by the non-fascist.[46] Mangan's work will develop further this aspect of sport and militarism in the future.

Power

The notion of power is inextricably intertwined with the notions of ideology, political socialization and narratives and constitutes a key element in our understanding of the relationship between militarism and civil society. In their analysis of the historical sociology of war, Martin Shaw and Colin Creighton contended that

> the state is the social institution which explains the dichotomous relationship of modern societies to violence. The experience which we have been discussing, in which the scope of war has widened while the legitimate violence within society has narrowed, has its roots in the state's ever more successful assertion of its legal monopoly of force.[47]

The peculiar role of the state in legitimizing violence can be seen in the use of athleticism for transforming boys' brutal pastime practices such as killing animals for pleasure into channelled aggression and violence in the form of sports and games – but which, when necessary, could be directed towards defending the state's interests on a battlefield.

Mangan's critical historicism has been concerned mainly with two different conceptions of power: (i) as circulated through the relations of knowledge for the constructing of identities, and (ii) as structural relations in constructing schooling (e.g, via class, ethnicity or gender). The first conception of power emphasizes the construction of national identities. Nation states, as Michael Mann has maintained, are *citizen* states, which consist of a political community of free, participating citizens.[48] What connects this mass citizenship within a given territory to war and militarism is the surge of nationalism. The material form of the state, claims Ahrne,[49] is of great importance for understanding social processes. Hence the concepts of terrain, territoriality and people become essential elements of a social landscape (Ahrne's metaphor for society), predetermining the nature of social interactions. The modern (Western) state, however, is not single but dual; that is, it has both well defined and separated domestic and geopolitical forms. Subsequently, Marxist, liberal and militarist schools have promoted different views of the state. The state, as depicted in Mangan's analysis, appears to be of liberal type as it mediates systematically between upper-middle and working classes in asserting various models of sport while trying to reconcile different interests. In addition, because of its imperialist aspirations, the British state was equally concerned with promoting its national and racial interests, a view held by the military school. The important point here is that, given the dual form of the state (the separability and mutual reinforcement of its domestic and geopolitical interests), militarism and sport were used to establish a class balance, and even more importantly to move the ideological, political, economic and military powers of the state in the same direction to achieve synergy, or what Hall calls 'enabling power',[50] in the pursuit of the state hegemonic project.

The construction and dissemination of knowledge played an important part in this process. Mangan, with the help of other scholars, has carefully documented the educational policies of state and local educational boards. The role of textbooks, educational certificates, the organization of curriculum and a system of rituals in the making of imperialist mentalities have all come under his scrutiny. Textbooks painted a typical picture of the British Empire as 'a moral enterprise; an imperial ethic constructed around the notion of "character"; an emphasis on the moral deficiency of subjected people; and the categorization of superior and inferior into a "hierarchy of race"'.[51] Mark Moss' analysis of young boys' education in Ontario (1870–1914) also made this point plainly. As he demonstrated, the key message of *Ontario High School History of England* was that England was always right. Imperialism was justified because it brought civilization to the heathen, and boys were to become brave and honourable men.[52] The 'right' knowledge was, of course, to be found primarily in schools which, borrowing from the 'garrison state' analogy, Mangan referred to as '"moral garrisons"', positioned at strategic points in a sustained cultural assault'.[53]

Two examples, representing different levels of perception and manifestation of identities, will suffice to illustrate the process of identity construction. The first is at the level of the nation-state, 'people-as-one' image captured by the Canadian Prime Minister's famous declaration in 1914 that 'when England is at war, Canada is at war'. The second is a testimony to the Victorian and Edwardian athletic tradition that prompted thousands of young sportsmen to volunteer to serve king and country. During the First World War, as Dennis Brailsford evidenced, 'Edgar Mobbs, Northampton and England rugby player, raised his own company of his county's sportsmen, and led an attack out of the trenches by kicking up a rugby ball high into No Man's Land and chasing forward to follow up.'[54] This exploit is still celebrated in the annual memorial match played between East Midlands and Barbarians teams.

Educational certificates, of course, validated that the 'right' knowledge was acquired, which Stockwell terms instruments of 'imperial management'. These certificates emerged as 'the passport to local employment in government, commerce and the professions',[55] particularly in the colonies. Sathyamurthy has made the relationship between knowledge and the construction of identities in India even more explicit. He asserts that 'the lure of the English language as well as the content of English education have to date been irresistible to the Indian ruling classes. It has continued to govern their intellectual, institutional and ideological preferences.'[56] The fact that the English language was given preference over classical oriental languages because of its great practical utility illustrates the connection between the acquisition of modern knowledge and asserting one's status in society. This connection is, of course, much subtler and deeply rooted, as Jurgen Habermas's critical analysis of knowledge and human interest demonstrated. The imposition of particular knowledge or a language on the part of those in power results inevitably in what Habermas called a systematic distortion of communication, which is a condition of the emancipatory interest.[57] The promotion of athleticism and the English language (as medium for teaching, a world-view and an achievement in itself) paved the way for the emergence of new social forces both in Britain and in the empire. Mangan was among the first, in his *Athleticism*, to explore the relationship between language, sport and socialization.

The dissemination of the 'right' knowledge was critically assisted by a carefully crafted and maintained powerful system of rituals involving physical action or embodiment. Mangan sees rituals as having several important social functions and concludes that they 'help develop, promote and reinforce feelings which determine roles and role playing in society'.[58] Here, he employs a semiological (although not fully fledged) analysis of cultural practices to unveil the meaning they convey. Together with other contributors he examines the significance of mass events and celebrations for asserting the relationship between imperialist identities, status and knowledge. Organizing displays with 'large numbers of children dressed in red, white and blue, forming living Union Jacks, and at which they were exhorted to be brave, loyal imperialists, proud of city, country and Empire'[59] became regular occurrences at the end of the nineteenth century. The pinnacle of these events was Empire Day, the first official celebration of which was held in 1904. Its message, Anne Bloomfield observes, 'was to convey the importance of British imperialism and to further the cause of Empire through the veneration and perpetuation of honourable British traditions and privileges'.[60]

Closely intertwined with the concept of power, as circulated through the relations of knowledge for constructing identities, is the second meaning of power as structural relations in constructing schooling in terms of class, ethnicity and gender. Lord Macaulay's famous minute eloquently set out these relations as early as 1835:

> I feel . . . that it is impossible for us, with our limited means, to attempt to educate the body of the people. We must at present do our best to form a class of persons, Indian in blood and colour but English in taste, in opinion, in morals and in intellect.[61]

Thus the provision of education and the organization of schooling followed a similar agenda. Since militarism needs male soldiers, it offers a 'natural' divide between boys and girls and plays an important role in the construction of gender. The imperial 'womanliness' envisaged that girls were charged with domestic duties 'keeping the home fire burning' but underpinned with the necessary patriotism for home defence. Squadron Leader Beryl Escott demonstrated, in *Twentieth Century Women of Courage*,[62] that imperial women's war exploits were not in short supply. The construction of schooling, however, never followed a clear path and involved at times both processes of enculturation (an aggressive induction into the dominant culture) and acculturation (a passive acquisition of elements of culture). Schools provided the environment for young boys and girls to mingle with the right people, to learn and to reproduce imperial mentalities. Without questioning the meaning of educational certificates discussed above, schools offered something more, which certificates did not show. To illustrate this point Mangan borrows from the sensible words of Musgrove:

> It is not the educational certificates but testimonials and referees' reports which get you into Boodle's and Brookes's, the Foreign Service, a merchant bank or the Household Cavalry. And testimonials tell the other story, of one's showing in the extra curriculum: which is bloody, non-literate, concrete, pragmatic, corporate and even convivial, bloody and applied.[63]

Perhaps Mangan's most explicit engagement with power, identities, state and sport is in his two-volume study of the fascist body as a political icon. Here perceptions of the male body, political ideology, effective action and state superiority all merge together. The dialectics of fascist socialization, according to Mangan, is simple: 'Sport develops muscle and muscle is equated with power – literally and metaphorically. War, the essence of Fascism, demands physical fitness and sport helps promote this fitness. Competitive sport can help develop attitudes of aggression and aggression is essential in war.'[64] These two volumes document in great detail the penetration of fascist ideology and practices in Europe, South America and Asia and provide ample evidence for the relationship between sport and militarism in asserting the nation state, hegemonic projects, power and identities.

Narratives

Mangan's examinations of imperial militarism are not confined to ideological and sporting rituals seen as a sign system. He has systematically deconstructed historical narratives into a set of functions and transformed this otherwise structuralist technique into a critical historicism by relating the narrative functions to the prevailing social and economic structure. Thus the social meaning of photographs, school documents and magazines, parents' accounts, national and local press, books and articles become manifested. The most prominent of these manifestations was the 'invention of tradition' – 'a set of practices, normally governed by overtly or tacitly accepted rules and of a ritual or symbolic nature, which seek to inculcate certain values and norms of behaviour by repetition, which automatically implies continuity with the past'.[65] One does not have to look hard to find proof of this statement. A brief examination of *The Theory of Physical Education* (1895) and *Raising the Game*, a recent government sport policy paper (1995), will suffice. Published exactly one hundred years apart, the following extracts bear witness to the invention and continuation of tradition:

> Boys' games exercise a powerful influence in forming individual character. They promote good temper, self-control, self-reliance, endurance, patience, courage under defeat, promptness and rapid judgement. . . . Much of the success in after life may be attributed to the qualities developed in boyhood, by the healthy, spirited games of school life.[66]

> Sport . . . through competition, [can] teach lessons which last for life; be a means of learning how to be both a winner and a loser; thrive only if 'both parties play by the rules', and accept the outcome 'with good grace'; teach how to live with others as part of a team; improve health; create friendships.[67]

A recent study has pointed out the contribution of athleticism to the growth of modern sport, 'the vehicle for the inculcation of these values [promoted by *Raising the Game* – my elaboration] were "our great traditional sports – cricket, hockey, swimming, athletics, football, netball, rugby, tennis and the like" – an explicit acknowledgement of the moral values long attributed to the playing field and above all to team games'.[68] In passing the authors praise Mangan's knowledge and unique contribution to the wider understanding of this relationship.

At a general level, by locating the role of English playing fields (seen as training grounds for imperial battlefields) in the context of British hegemonic imperialism, it becomes possible to map out the relationship between sport and imperial militarism. Mangan's analysis of various textbooks, schoolboys' doggerel, parents' letters and school magazines is presented as communications from influential groups in society (typically representatives of the upper class not only in Britain but across the empire) to young people in particular about what values they must subscribe to and how they should act. He shows, for example, how textbooks are structured around the continuous repetition of certain imperial racist themes of the British Empire as a moral enterprise that builds character and introduces it, in a 'top-down' manner, to those inferior peoples with a moral deficiency. In doing this, the textbooks contribute to constructing the imperial myth promoting the world-view of the dominant, and establishing the legitimacy of imperialization.

Equally instructive is Mangan's analysis of school budgets and magazines. The elitist character of education in public schools and its role in promoting the 'high culture' concept of athleticism is demonstrated by a reference to school spending on developing games facilities. He points out that in 1873 Harrow, one of the leading public schools, spent £4,000 on a new gymnasium compared, at the same time, to a modest government investment of £20,000 on educating the poor (read elementary schools). One of the the magazines' main functions was to monitor the evolution of masculinity at the universities. The narrative, in the form of verbal barbs, presents athletic pursuits as easily grasped binary oppositions, along the line of intellectual–anti-intellectual. On the other hand, by examining and comparing the main themes of schoolboys' doggerel, Mangan is able to demonstrate class differences and mentalities between the affluent, celebrating 'fair play', and the poor, promoting 'artful' means of winning useful prizes.[69]

A critical reading of parents' letters to their public schoolboy sons further reinforces the class divide and identity constructions. Mangan uses one father's exclamation, 'a man is known by the company he keeps',[70] after a horrific discovery that his son was reading *The Gem* and *The Magnet*, weekly comics for elementary school children, to convey a clear message of what is right and wrong for a young boy with an affluent upbringing. This company, according to the public-school ethos, had to nurture a constant flow of athletic warriors whose mission, as a youthful poet in the *Cheltonian* put it, was to perpetuate the Empire:

> *Neath old England's banner in every land,*
> *Our football players to guard it, stand.*[71]

Mangan also relates the narratives produced by state bodies (for example, the Public School Commission) and the national press to demonstrate how the ideal of the imperial gentleman was sanctioned and publicized. In the case of the former, it was done through a series of carefully worded, acceptable images, while in the latter, it was through a simultaneous denial of the modern range of sporting superstars and the glamorization of the athletic public schoolboy. Moreover, the deconstruction of narratives into set of functions allowed readers to comprehend the complex interplay between publicly discussed ideas and institutions, presenting them in rituals and introducing them as rules and norms to be acquired by the young. This also shows how the values of imperial militarism have constrained public policy and have performed the ideological work with material consequences for sport. To use the comment of Douglas Bland in his *Unified Theory of Civil-Military Relations*, 'ideas have influence on politics through their incorporation into the terms of the political debate'.[72] So have words and images!

THE PURSUIT OF THE DEMOCRATIC SOLDIER CONTINUES: TOWARDS A 'SPECTATOR SPORT MILITARISM'

Throughout this contribution, the engagement of J.A. Mangan with imperial militarism and sport during the Victorian, Edwardian and fascist eras has been examined. Attention has been given to his main approach of critical historicism. I have demonstrated that Mangan's work has systematically traced the complex relations between evolving democratic societies and military thinking and practices, and outlined the role of sport in the process of socializing young boys (and now girls). But how relevant is the pursuit of the democratic soldier, or the civil-military nexus in sport today after the ending of the cold war? Surely there must be a degree of continuity, but the imperial-militaristic sentiment of these bygone eras is no longer relevant to twenty-first-century geopolitical realities and societies. In the process of answering this question, the rest of this section will, I believe, be able to suggest some issues for a future research agenda. Moreover, the theme of continuity has always been central to Mangan's explorations of the subject.

Borrrowing Richard Keeble's 'From militarism to new militarism'[73] helps us to establish the main link between the militarism of the late nineteenth and early twentieth century and that of modern warfare. This link presents a continuation of the ongoing debate about the civil and military elements in society. The end of the Second World War posed some serious democratic dilemmas for Western elites. These included a simultaneous discrediting of old elites for collaborating with the Nazis and the rise of progressive and trade union movements. Subsequently, the idea of mass conscription in Britain was abandoned in 1963 as undemocratic and gradually replaced by a professional army with nuclear capability. The big change that signalled the shift from militarism to new militarism involved a growing separation of the state and military establishments from the public that was inherently anti-democratic. As Martin Shaw has argued, 'the state would dispense with the people in a future war, it had largely dispensed with the pretence of involving them in preparing for war too'.[74] But not only that. The separation was accompanied by a transformation of military strategies into media events, yet ones surrounded by great secrecy, which in the UK is ensured by more than 100 laws prohibiting the disclosure of information. This process was clearly demonstrated during the televised public debates in Britain *NATO on Trial* and *Afghan Strikes on Trial* (in relation to the Kosovo and Afghanistan situations in 2000 and 2001 respectively), in which the overwhelming majority of the British public categorically condemned military actions and called for a peaceful solution of these conflicts.

During Victorian times, as Mangan has demonstrated, working-, middle- and upper-class boys (and their parents too) were connected with the military's ideas and practices through a range of institutions and activities, including schools, churches, rituals and organized sports. The difference was that the Victorian newspapers, despite their power, did not have the social penetration of modern high-tech mass media. The force shaping the new militarism was, as Richard Keeble observes, that 'by the 1970s this institutional and social militarism had given way to a new mediacentric, consumerist, entertainment militarism in which the mass media, ideologically aligned to a strong and increasingly secretive state, had assumed a dominant ideological role'.[75] It is no wonder that the glamorized public schoolboy and the Nazi super-warrior have been replaced by images of the lone, hungry and cold but undefeated British SAS soldier (at least in Andy McNab's best-selling story of the lost SAS patrol in the Gulf War) or by his American counterpart hero Rambo, to which Mangan refers in the Epilogue of the first volume of *Shaping the Superman.*

This new militarism, to use Michael Mann's eloquent metaphor, is 'spectator sport militarism'. For critics who would find Mann's words somehow unsubstantiated, it might be useful to consider Steve Peak's observation that the Falklands War was the 88th deployment of British troops (in 51 countries) since 1945.[76] To round up this figure to at least 90 we only have to add the recent deployments in Kosovo and Afghanistan. The relationship of this kind of war to sport is one of substance. To quote Mann again:

> Wars like the Falklands or the Grenadan invasion are not qualitatively different from the Olympic Games. Because life and death are involved the emotions stirred up are deeper and stronger. But they are not emotions backed up by committing personal resources. They do not involve real or potential sacrifice, except by professional troops. The nuclear and mass conventional confrontation involves at most 10 per cent of GNP – a tithe paid to our modern 'church', the nation. The symbolic strength of the nation can sustain popular support for adventures and arms spending.[77]

Clearly, the new militarism is changing the relationships between civil and military elements in society and men and women, but the main issues of ideology, power, masculinity and narratives remain. The military-masculinity link, thoroughly investigated by Mangan, can no longer operate in quite the same way as it did in the last two centuries. One area which appears to be heavily affected by the modern transformation of militarism is the managerialization of the public sector. It is worth considering the sensitive warning of John Hopton who argued that since the late 1980s the emerging management ideologies 'have the potential to replace militarism as a mechanism of social control – especially at the level of ideology'.[78] What concerns Hopton is the unproblematic and subtle transfer of military concepts into the public domain through management theories that promote and consolidate traditional masculinist values. Examples include the equation of the vital figure of the heroic risk-taking manager with the individual heroic warrior, the priority of expanding 'market shares' and 'dominating markets' with traditional military concerns of winning and defending territories, or civil organizations' preoccupations with corporate logos, clothing and identity – resonating closely with regimental practices or, for that matter, tribal identities, to which Mangan has devoted many publications.[79]

Moving to the application of managerialism in sport, Girginov has argued recently that the study of masculinity, which is a constituent element of militarism, has four major implications for sports policy analysis: first, that masculinity changes over time and there are always dominant and emergent masculinities; second, the cultural dimension of masculinity has an emphasis on the use of human bodies as instruments of our wills; third, masculinity has a subjective character as a social construct but is organized within structures of control and authority, and fourth, that masculinity, like most social phenomena, produces its own paradoxes by giving birth to social movements that seek to diminish its power.[80]

There is little doubt that the pursuit of the democratic soldier continues. Neither militarism nor sports are static entities. As both evolve and change over time, new avenues for investigation emerge. John Harris's review of *Shaping the Superman: Fascist Body as Political Icon: Aryan Fascism* in the *European Sport Management Quarterly*[81] was indicative of a growing sensitivity in sport management students towards studies on the relationship between sport and militarism. He identified three areas of direct relation between militarism and sport which fit into Mann's notion of 'spectator sport militarism'. These are paralleled by the growing gap between the popularity of spectator sport and the decline of participation and could be seen also as research issues. They are: (i) the warrior and the athlete as symbols of national prowess and their importance in the study of the role of the state in sport and sport organizations; (ii) a changing emphasis in national identity in sport from an exclusively male affair to 'one that places an increasing currency on the performance of female athletes'; and (iii) a resurrected nationalism and the use of the male body by state agencies in promoting particular political ideologies and management practices affecting the work of sport organizations. In addition to sport management/policy, three more areas hold promise for future investigations: (i) the relationship between state-building, warfare and sport in an increasingly globalized world; (ii) the use of military power in developing 'social capacity' in emerging societies, including their sports structures, and the legal and economic frameworks within which they operate, as in the case of NATO's current involvement in Kosovo; and (iii) the role of sport as antidote to militarism in preserving liberal freedoms and democracy. This is evidence that the intellectual inspiration of Mangan's work on the subject of militarism and sport over the past 30-odd years constitutes a lasting legacy.

NOTES

1. J.A. Mangan (ed.), *Making Imperial Mentalities: Socialisation and British Imperialism* (Manchester: Manchester University Press, 1990), p.20 (emphasis in original).
2. J.A. Mangan (ed.), *Militarism, Sport, Europe: War Without Weapons* (*The European Sports History Review*, 5) (London and Portland, OR: Frank Cass, 2003).
3. J.A. Mangan and C. McKenzie, *Blooding the Male: Masculinity, Fieldsports, Hunting and Militarism* (London and Portland, OR: Frank Cass, forthcoming).
4. J.A. Mangan, *Athleticism in the Victorian and Edwardian Public School: The Emergence and Consolidation of an Educational Ideology*, 2nd edn (London and Portland, OR: Frank Cass, 2000), p.5.
5. James Toner, *The American Military Ethic: A Mediation* (New York: Praeger, 1992), p.225.
6. Samuel Huntington, *The Soldier and The State* (Cambridge, MA: The Belknap Press of Harvard University Press, 1957), p.79.
7. Quoted in Volker Berghahn, *Militarism: The History of an International Debate 1861–1979* (Leamington Spa: Berg, 1981), p.7.
8. Ibid., p.8 (emphasis in original).
9. Michael Klare, 'Militarism: The Issues Today', in A. Eide and M. Thee (eds), *Problems of Contemporary Militarism* (London: Croom Helm, 1980), p.36.
10. For an extended discussion on German militarism see Nicholas Stargardt, *The German Idea of Militarism: Radical and Socialist Critics 1868–1914* (Cambridge: Cambridge University Press, 1994), p.79.
11. Ibid., p.101.
12. Ibid., p.2.
13. Quoted in Berghahn, *Militarism*, p.8.
14. See D. Wilshire, *The Social and Political Thought of Herbert Spencer* (Oxford: Oxford University Press, 1978).
15. Niall Ferguson, *The Pity of War* (London: Penguin Books, 1998), p.15.
16. Alex Callinicos, *Making History. Agency, Structure and Change in Social Theory* (London: Polity Press, 1995), p.169.
17. Quoted in ibid., p.168.
18. Hew Strachan, *The Politics of the British Army* (Oxford and New York: Clarendon Press, 1997).
19. Paul Smith, *Government and Armed Forces in Britain 1856–1990* (London, OH: Hambleden Press, 1996).
20. Alfred Vagts, *A History of Militarism. Romance and Realities of a Profession* (London, 1938).
21. Stargardt, *The German Idea of Militarism*, pp.13–14.
22. Berghahn, *Militarism*, pp.2–3.
23. Marek Thee, 'Militarism and Militarisation in Contemporary International Relations', in Eide and Thee, *Problems of Contemporary Militarism*, p.19.
24. J.A. Mangan (ed.), *Shaping the Superman: Fascist Body as Political Icon – Aryan Fascism* (London and Portland, OR: Frank Cass, 1999), pp.180–195.
25. John MacKenzie, *Propaganda and Empire: The Manipulation of British Public Opinion*

1880–1960 (Manchester: Manchester University Press, 1984).

26. J.A. Mangan (ed.), *Militarism, Sport, Europe: War Without Weapons* (London and Portland, OR: Frank Cass, 2003).

27. See Richard Holt, *Sport and the British: A Modern History* (Oxford: Oxford University Press, 1989), and H. Meinander and J.A. Mangan (eds), *The Nordic World* (London and Portland, OR: Frank Cass, 2000).

28. Personal communication, 10 December 2001.

29. Lee Harvey, *Critical Social Research* (London: Unwin Hyman, 1990), p.26.

30. Alun Munslow, 'History in Focus: What is History?' 2 (2001), online at http://ihr.sas.ac.uk/ihr/Focus/Whatishistory/, p.4 (accessed 11 Dec. 2001).

31. Mangan, *Athleticism in the Victorian and Edwardian Public School*, p.3.

32. Harvey, *Critical Social Research*, pp.27, 28.

33. Thomas Popkewitz, 'Whose Future? Whose Past? Notes on Critical Theory and Methodology', in E.G. Guba (ed.), *The Paradigm Dialog* (Newbury Park, CA: Sage, 1990), p.30.

34. Mangan, *Athleticism in the Victorian and Edwardian Public School*, 28, p.6.

35. Ibid., p.9.

36. Mangan, *Making Imperial Mentalities*, p.19.

37. J.A. Mangan and C. Hickey, 'English Elementary Education: Revisited and Revised: Drill and Athleticism in Tandem', in J.A. Mangan (ed.), *Sport in Europe. Politics, Class, Gender (The European Sports History Review*, 1) (London and Portland, OR: Frank Cass, 1999), p.88.

38. Bob Jessop, 'Accumulation Strategies, State Forms and Hegemonic Projects', in S. Clarke (ed.), *The State Debate* (London: Macmillan, 1991), p.171.

39. Robert Brenner quoted in Callinicos, *Making History*, p.162 (emphasis in Brenner's original).

40. Ian Henry, *The Politics of Leisure Policy*, 2nd edn (Houndmills: Palgrave, 2001), p.12.

41. Popkewitz, 'Whose Future? Whose Past?, p.30.

42. Don Anthony, *Minds, Bodies and Souls. An Archaeology of the Olympic Heritage Network* (London: British Olympic Association, 1999), p.37.

43. P.M. McIntosh, 'Physical Education in England Since 1800' quoted in Don Anthony, *Minds, Bodies and Souls: An Archaeology of the Olympic Heritage Network* (London: BOA, 1999), p.51.

44. Mangan and Hickey, 'English Elementary Education', p.72.

45. As documented by Don Anthony, *Minds, Bodies and Souls*, p.52.

46. J.A. Mangan, 'Global Fascism and the Male Body: Ambitions, Similarities and Dissimilarities', in J.A. Mangan (ed.), *'Superman Supreme: Fascist Body as Political Icon: Global Fascism* (London and Portland, OR: Frank Cass, 2000), p.2.

47. M. Shaw and C. Creighton, 'Introduction', in C. Creighton and M. Shaw (eds), *The Sociology of War and Peace* (Houndmills: Macmillan Press, 1987), p.5.

48. M. Mann, 'War and Social Theory: Into Battle with Classes, Nations and States', in Creighton and Shaw, *The Sociology of War and Peace*, p.58.

49. Goran Ahrne, *Agency and Organisations: Towards an Organisational Theory of Society* (London: Sage, 1990), pp.24–6.

50. A. Hall, 'How Should We Theorise Sport in a Capitalist Patriarchy?', *International Review for the Sociology of Sport*, 20, 1/2, 41–58.

51. Mangan, *Making Imperial Mentalities*, p.14.

52. Mark Moss, *Manliness and Militarism: Educating Young Boys in Ontario for War* (Toronto: University of Toronto Press, 1999).

53. Mangan, *Making Imperial Mentalities*, p.15.

54. Dennis Brailsford, *British Sport: A Social History* (Cambridge: Lutterworth Press, 1992), p.123.

55. A.J. Stockwell, 'Examinations and Empire: The Cambridge Certificate in the colonies, 1857–1957', in Mangan (ed.), *Making Imperial Mentalities*, p.203.

56. T.V. Sathyamurthy, 'Victorians, Socialisation and Imperialism: Consequences for Post-imperial India', in Mangan, *Making Imperial Mentalities*, p.112.

57. For an extended discussion on knowledge, interest and social action see J. Habermas, *Knowledge and Human Interest* (London: Heinemann, 1972) and *The Theory of Communicative*

Action, Vol.2 (Boston, MA: Beacon Press, 1987).

58. J.A. Mangan and C. Hickey, 'Athleticism in the Service of the Proletariat: Preparation for the English Elementary School and the Extension of Middle-Class Manliness', in J.A. Mangan (ed.), *Making European Masculinities: Sport, Europe, Gender* (*The European Sports History Review*, 2) (London and Portland, OR: Frank Cass, 2000), p.126.

59. Mangan, *Making Imperial Mentalities*, p.8.

60. A. Bloomfield, 'Drill and Dance as Symbols of Imperialism', in Mangan, *Making Imperial Mentalities*, p.74.

61. Quoted in Sathyamurthy, 'Victorians, Socialisation and Imperialism', p.110.

62. Beryl Escott, *Twentieth Century Women of Courage* (Stroud: Sutton Publishing, 1999).

63. Quoted in Mangan, *Making Imperial Mentalities*, p.18.

64. J.A. Mangan, 'Global Fascism and the Male Body: Ambitions, Similarities and Dissimilarities', in Mangan, *Superman Supreme*, p.1, see also J.A. Mangan (ed.), *Shaping the Superman: Fascist Body as Political Icon: Aryan Fascism* (London and Portland, OR: Frank Cass, 1999).

65. Mangan and Hickey, 'Athleticism in the Service of the Proletariat', p.131.

66. Quoted in ibid., p.71.

67. Department of National Heritage, *Raising the Game* (London, 1995), p.2.

68. J. Horne, A. Tomlinson and G. Whannel, *Understanding Sport: An Introduction to the Sociological and Cultural Analysis of Sport* (London: E & FN Spon, 1999), p.12.

69. See for example Mangan's analysis of 'The Sports' in Mangan and Hickey, 'English Elementary Education', p.84.

70. Quoted in Mangan and Hickey, 'English Elementary Education', p.86.

71. Mangan, *Athleticism in the Victorian and Edwardian Public School*, p.138.

72. D. Bland, 'A Unified Theory of Civil-Military Relations', *Armed Forces & Society*, 26, 1 (Fall 1999), p.5.

73. R. Keeble, *Secret State, Silent Press. New Militarism, the Gulf and the Modern Image of Warfare* (Luton: University of Luton Press, 1997), p.6.

74. M. Shaw, 'Rise and Fall of the Military-democratic State 1940–1985', in Creighton and Shaw, *The Sociology of War and Peace*, p.153.

75. Keeble, *Secret State, Silent Press*, p.9.

76. Quoted in ibid., p.15.

77. Quoted in ibid., p.10.

78. J. Hopton, 'Militarism, Masculinism and Managerialisation in the British Public Sector', *Journal of Gender Studies*, 8, 1 (1999), 72.

79. See for example the most comprehensive of these: J.A. Mangan (ed), *Tribal Identities; Nationalism, Europe, Sport* (London and Portland, OR: Frank Cass, 1996).

80. V. Girginov, 'Pre-Totalitarian, Totalitarian and Post-Totalitarian Masculinity: The Projection of the Male Image in Sports Policy in Bulgaria', in Mangan, *Making European Masculinities*, pp.160–84.

81. J. Harris, review of *Shaping the Superman*, *European Sport Management Quarterly*, 1, 1 (2001), 79–80.

Sport in the Global Society:
Shaping the Domain of Sport Studies

TREVOR SLACK

One of the indicators of the strength of an academic discipline, or sub-discipline, is the quantity and quality of the literature by which it is underpinned. In the last few years the socio-cultural and historical areas of sport have been considerably strengthened by the growth of the Frank Cass book series 'Sport in the Global Society'. While other publishers have produced book series devoted to the social science areas of sport, none have been as prolific or developed as rapidly as the Cass series.[1] The most current Cass catalogue lists 76 titles in press or in print, all but six with a post 1995 publication date.[2] The series is of course driven by Tony Mangan who, in addition to being series editor, has also been editor, co-editor, author or contributor to several of the books. The series began in 1997. Mangan had previously edited a series with Manchester University Press entitled 'International Studies in the History of Sport'. Concerned about the narrowness of the scope of the MUP series and with his agreement with them coming to an end, Mangan approached Frank Cass. Enthusiastic about the explosion in sport studies, Cass saw the potential in the market and subsequently the 'Sport in the Global Society' series was born.

The aim of the initiative was to produce the leading book series in the social science aspects of sport studies. As the current Frank Cass catalogue notes, 'the series is unique. It draws together many subjects in the expanding study of sport in the global society, providing comprehensiveness and comparison within a single series.'[3] In a recent conversation, Mangan told me that some of his history colleagues 'warned him off' attempting such a wide-ranging task that focused on sport. But the man whom cultural historian Jeffrey Richards described as a cross between a bishop and a prize-fighter[4] (although

Richards acknowledged he had not seen a lot of the bishop!) is not easily swayed and does not shy away from such challenges.

Mangan's aim was to move away from a sole focus on cultural history to a more comprehensive set of books that would focus on broader topics within the social sciences. The early texts in the series, however, stayed close to Mangan's own personal writing programme and to his interest in cultural history. The first book in the series *Footbinding, Feminism and Freedom: The Liberation of Women's Bodies in Modern China* chronicles the physical emancipation of Chinese women.[5] Written by Fan Hong, it exemplifies what for me are two of the main qualities of the 'Sport in the Global Society' series: the involvement of young scholars and the focus on previously neglected topics, points I will return to later. The second book in the series was a reissued version of Mangan's own 1986 text *The Games Ethic and Imperialism: Aspects of the Diffusion of an Ideal*, a sequel to his 1981 *Athleticism in the Victorian and Edwardian Public School*. Mangan's presence is also found in the third of the series, an edited collection with Henrik Meinander entitled *The Nordic World: Sport in Society*.

As the series has grown the emphasis has, as Mangan intended, moved away from a singular focus on cultural history to a broader set of topics. The most recent Frank Cass catalogue groups the contents of the series under ten headings – Soccer; Rugby; Cricket; Gender; Nationalisms, Nations and Identity; British Sport; European Sport; World Sport; Professionalization and Commercialization of Sport; and Sport and the Law. In an attempt to increase the availability of the works, several of the volumes within the series have also been distributed as special issues of Cass journals. For example Darby, Johnes and Mellor's *Soccer and Disaster* appeared as a special issue of the journal *Soccer and Society*; Dauncey and Hare's *France and the 1998 World Cup* appeared as a special issue of *Culture, Sport, Society* and Cronin and Mayall's *Sporting Nationalisms: Identity, Ethnicity, Immigration and Assimilation* as a special issue of *Immigrants and Minorities*. While there may be those who take issue with such practice, the dwindling resources of libraries provide an inherent logic for making specific journals available in cheaper book form.

For me, there are a number of distinguishing features of the series that make it stand out as one of the most significant contributions to the social scientific study of sport. First is the diversity and quality of authors that have either written texts or contributed to edited volumes;

Pierre Bourdieu,[6] Ann Hall,[7] David Andrews,[8] John Bale,[9] Eric Dunning,[10] Wray Vamplew,[11] Steve Redhead,[12] Gertrud Pfister,[13] Douglas Booth[14] and Patricia Vertinsky[15] are just a few of the names who have contributed books or chapters (in some cases more than one) and by any standards are leaders in their field. However, the list of authors is not just limited to academics. Gordon Taylor,[16] chief executive of the Professional Footballers' Association, Chris Smith,[17] former Secretary of State for Culture, Media and Sport, and Sir Alex Ferguson,[18] manager of Manchester United, have all made contributions to books in the series. Coupled with others who have either authored books or contributed to edited collections, the list of writers involved in 'Sport in the Global Society' reads like a *Who's Who* of the socio-cultural study of sport.

However, it is not just the established authors to whom Mangan has directed his attention in seeking contributors. He has also been instrumental in giving a helping hand to the careers of new scholars; in creating an awareness, in the English-speaking world, of the work of scholars from countries where the first language is not English; and in encouraging academics whose main focus is not sport to write about this topic. Fan Hong[19] and Dong Jinxia[20] were both PhD students of Mangan, and Paul Dimeo[21] completed his PhD at Strathclyde where Mangan is based. All three published in the 'Sport in the Global Society' series shortly after the completion of their PhD studies. For Fan Hong (*Footbinding, Feminism and Freedom*) and Dong Jinxia, their books emanated directly from their doctoral work. Andrew Ritchie, a current doctoral student of Mangan, has a book entitled *Bicycle Racing: Sport, Technology and Modernity, 1869–1903*, based on his PhD work, scheduled to appear in 2003. Other doctoral students of Mangan's who are publishing, or have published, with Cass include Colm Hickey, Hamad S. Ndee, and Callum McKenzie.

In his efforts to expand the global reach of the socio-cultural study of sport Mangan has also actively encouraged scholars from countries where the native language is something other than English to publish their research in the 'Sport in the Global Society' series. This aim is perhaps best articulated in Mangan's foreword to Dimeo and Mills' *Soccer in South Asia*, where he suggests, with a specific regard to Asia, that 'Asian voices in English are still in too short supply in academia'. In future volumes of the series, 'Eastern voices will speak for themselves; Eastern commentators will advance Western perspectives on Asia'.

Mangan's focus is not just on Asia, however; the Nordic countries, continental Europe and Latin America have all been targeted with the same intent and a quick scan at the contents page of such edited collections as *The Nordic World: Sport in Society* (Meinander and Mangan), *Reformers, Sport, Modernizers* (Mangan) and *Sport in Latin American Society: Past and Present* (Mangan and DaCosta) will demonstrate the success that Mangan has had in moving our understanding of social issues in sport away from a perspective that has been primarily Anglo-American in orientation. This is in direct contrast with most of the other major book series (SUNY Press, University of Illinois, University of Minnesota) where the emphasis is decidedly North American.[22] Broadening the range of literature for those of us who work in the social science area of sport provides a basis from which to challenge many of the normative assumptions that we make when our theoretical and methodological perspectives are clearly entrenched in a body of work limited in scope to a focus on Britain and North America, primarily the US.

As series editor Mangan has also been successful in attracting scholars who have not traditionally written about sport to engage with the field. Dauncey and Hare, for example, are both senior lecturers in French at the University of Newcastle upon Tyne and with the exception of their book *France and the 1998 World Cup* (and another Cass book about the Tour de France on the way[23]), they have not published extensively in the sport studies field.[24] Likewise neither Peter J. Beck, a professor of international history at Kingston University, UK, and author of *Scoring for Britain: International Football and International Politics, 1900–1939* and Andrew Hignell, a geography teacher at Wells Cathedral School in Somerset and author of *Rain Stops Play: Cricketing Climates*, had written in the area of sport prior to their involvement with Cass. However, both exhibited a deep personal interest in their sport and with Mangan's encouragement contributed to the 'Sport in the Global Society' series, thus sharing the benefits of their knowledge.

'Sport in the Global Society' also makes a significant contribution to the field in that it has opened up a number of areas of study which were previously relatively unexplored. For example, as the world looks forward to the 2008 Olympic Games in Beijing, the Cass series provides us with what are the two of the first books in English written by Chinese nationals.[25] While several English-language books have been produced on China[26] none has brought the insights and access to original Chinese sources that are found in *Footbinding, Feminism and Freedom* and *Women, Sport and Society in Modern China*. By being given access to data that have hitherto been inaccessible to Western scholars interested in China, those working in this area are helped enormously. Similar claims could also be made for texts such as Dimeo and Mills' *Soccer in South Asia*, Dauncey and Hare's *France and the 1998 World Cup*, Meinander and Mangan's *The Nordic World*, Mangan, Holt and Lanfranchi's *European Heroes* and Mangan and DaCosta's *Sport in Latin American Society*. Each of these volumes contains a number of articles that provide information previously limited to those who had the required language skills and/or the ability to access what are relatively hard to obtain data. As such, by being exposed to such writings our ethnocentric views are challenged and we are able to engage with a broader set of social constructions that influence sport.

Like China, Africa has, in recent years, seen increased involvement on the world sporting stage. With the return of South Africa to the international sport scene and the success of footballers from Cameroon and Senegal and runners from Kenya, Ethiopia, Morocco and Algeria, the Africa continent has become an established force in sport. Three of the texts in the 'Sport in the Global Society' series focus on Africa[27] and a fourth is due out in 2003.[28] The global scope of the Cass texts is captured in the range of other geographic areas that are covered in the series. Britain and more broadly Europe is covered in a number of ways;[29] Australia is specifically dealt with in Mangan and Nauright's *Sport in Australasian Society* and Douglas Booth's *Australian Beach Culture*; Asia in Mangan and Fan Hong's recently published *Sport in Asian Society: Past and Present*; New Zealand in Greg Ryan's forthcoming *The Making of New Zealand Cricket, 1832–1914*; Latin America in Mangan and DaCosta's *Sport in Latin American Society* and Matthias Röhrig Assunção's forthcoming *Capoeira: A History of an Afro-Brazilian Martial Art* and Japan in Maguire and Nakaya's forthcoming *Japan, Sport and Globalization*. In fact, the only geographic area which does not received extensive consideration within the series is North America[30] – which given the proliferation of social-science and historical books about sport on this continent is not a grave cause for concern.

The range and quality of books in the series has been recognized in a number of ways. At the 2001 celebration of 15 years of Cass books, sport sociologist Eric Dunning suggested that Frank Cass and specifically the

'Sport in the Global Society' series had helped make sport an academically viable area of study. Mangan's *Athleticism* was, he suggested, a landmark, and his *From 'Fair Sex' to Feminism: Sport and the Socialization of Women in the Industrial and Post-Industrial Eras* (co-edited with Roberta Park) 'path breaking'. This latter sentiment was echoed by Patricia Vertinsky in her review of the text, where she noted: 'By focusing substantially upon analysis rather than description the essays in this volume mark a watershed in scholarship on women's sport history'. Other texts have received similar accolades and awards: John Bale and Joe Sang's *Kenyan Running*, won the British Sport History Best Book prize in 1997 and Tony Collins' *Rugby's Great Split: Class Culture and the Origins of Rugby League Football* won the award in 1998. Douglas Booth's *The Race Game* won the North American Society for Sport History award in 1998 and Mike Huggins won this award for his *Flat Racing and British Society, 1790–1914* in 2001.

While the contributors to the series are among the best scholars in their field, there can be little doubt that the driving force behind the series is Tony Mangan. Those who know Tony will know that he has coaxed, coerced, and encouraged people he felt had something to say to put their ideas in print and make them a part of the series. In the course of his efforts to make the Cass series the tour de force that it is, he has personally edited work, rewritten sections, and provided suggestions for titles, cover pages and written numerous prologues. A personal anecdote will perhaps serve to illustrate Tony's drive and involvement in the series. Several years ago, when I was working at De Montfort University in England, Tony visited to give a talk to our students. I had known him for a number of years and of course knew about the Cass series. I approached him with the idea of a book on the commercialization of sport, as I felt that with the exception of Lawrence and Rowe's 1986 book *Power Play: Essays in the Sociology of Australian Sport* and a number of isolated chapters in texts, there was little on what was a highly visible and increasingly prevalent phenomenon. 'Great Idea, send me a proposal – nothing lengthy, just the main idea'. Well, like most academics I had a number of projects 'on the go' and although I was interested in the book it got pushed to the proverbial back-burner. But then the hastily written faxes started to come: 'No pressure, like the idea of the book, any progress?' 'Still waiting for the proposal, good topic, you're the person to do it'. Whether it was flattery, guilt, or gentle persuasion, the barely legible faxes kept coming as Tony encouraged me to pursue my ideas about the book. The text is now complete and we are finalizing the title and cover page. Tony is still involved, offering suggestions, faxing possible cover pages, and generally encouraging and supporting my efforts. I am sure that my work, like that of many other authors and contributors to the Cass series, would not have seen the light of day had it not been for what Jeffrey Richards described as Tony's proselytizing zeal and his energy and encouragement in promoting 'Sport in the Global Society'.

My own text, which will be entitled *Money, Sport, Markets: Commercialism and Corporations*, is somewhat of a new direction for the series in that, along with Steve Greenfield's and Guy Osborn's *Law and Sport in Contemporary Society* it falls into the area broadly termed sport management. This would appear, to me at least, to be a fruitful direction for future books in the 'Sport in the Global Society' series. As sport becomes increasingly linked with commercial practices, as the sport industry has grown to be a multibillion dollar business and companies such as Nike, IMG and News Corporation are more and more shaping the type of sport we watch and play, the intersections and interactions of sport and commerce become an ever more present set of topics in the sport studies programmes of universities and colleges. Many existing texts fail to look critically at these practices and the approach taken to scholarship in the Cass series has much to offer this area. Indeed, I have to confess that Mangan has seen this light too and volumes on both management and tourism are already being commissioned.

Mangan's original intention was to cover the range of topics that are within the socio-cultural and historical study of sport, and the future will see engagement with other developing fields. For example, the area of sport tourism is a growing and as yet relatively unexplored area where there is considerable room for work given its economic and social significance. Linked to the growth of sport tourism is an increased interest in sport events. These events range from such high-profile activities as the Olympics and Soccer World Cup to the World Police and Firefighters Games and the World Dwarf Games.[31] As scholars such as Roche[32] and Burbank, Andranovich and Heying[33] have shown, there is much to be studied about such events, including issues pertaining to urban regeneration, public policy and tourism. As such, this will be a useful area of expansion for the Cass series, given the global relevance of such issues. Key to the success of these events is their relationship with the media. Crolley's and Hands' *Football, Europe and the Press* and Alina Bernstein's and Neil Blain's *Sport, Media, Society* represent an initial incursion, for the Cass series, into the area of sport and the media, but there is much scope for work here. The globalizing force of companies such as News Corporation and the impact that the collapse of ITV Digital[34] and Kirch Media[35] has had on sport demonstrate the importance of the media in shaping the structure and operation of sport. University programmes in sport studies are increasingly including this area in their course offerings, thus creating a demand for a scholarly analysis of the relationship between sport and the media.

As Mangan points out in his foreword to *Soccer in South Asia*, there are also plans to expand the series to further address regional issues in sport. Specific areas on which he suggest there will be a focus include North America, which as I have noted has received relatively little attention, at least in this series, and Eastern Europe. Given the rapid transitions which are taking place in the latter, this region provides interesting material for studies of the way emerging economies are making the shift from a planned to a more market-led economy and the impact this is having on the structure and operation of sport. Other emerging economies, such as those in Africa, the Middle East and South America, could similarly provide useful sites of investigation and material for future works. One would expect that, as has been the tradition in the Cass series in the past, any works emanating from these areas will involve significant local input by native writers. Analyses of sport based in the literature of postmodernism[36] and cultural studies are also gaining popularity, and the 'Sport in the Global Society' series has yet to publish texts that engage with these perspectives. The broader acceptance of these approaches in the social sciences suggest that this also would be a fruitful area of expansion.

There is indeed much still to be done. Tony Mangan, through the 'Sport in the Global Society' series, has provided an incredibly strong foundation on which to move forward. He shows no signs of slowing down and as long as he has the opportunity to meet with his wide range of colleagues (and a fax machine!) I have little doubt he will continue to show the energy and enthusiasm he has in the past and to drive the series forward. It is difficult for one person to capture the impact that such a wide-ranging set of books as the Cass publications have had so it may be appropriate to conclude with some comments from others on some of the books within the series:

> [a book written with] originality, fluency and the capacity for challenging or even overturning established shibboleths. ... Essential reading for historians of sport and popular culture. ... Huggins alerts us to a balance of power in which the roughs often held better cards than the 'respectables' and sets up an impressive potential agenda for further research. This is a very important and enjoyable book.[37]

This book is essential, not only for the Nordic world but for other worlds. To the reviewer it answered several questions beyond the histories of the countries described. These questions arose between 1997 and 2000 when he was involved as an academic adviser to an EU [European Union] funded project investigating the post-1945 history of Austria, Denmark, Finland, Sweden and the United Kingdom. Many of the questions could now be answered after reading this inspiring collection. Editors and authors deserve much praise for the job they have done. Other regions apparently will be given consideration in future volumes of the laudable Cass series Sport in the Global Society – Australasia, Latin America and Eastern Europe, among others in the near future. *The Nordic World* provides the role model for such enterprises, both in content and in structure.[38]

Hong must be commended for her excellent job of chronicling Chinese women's physical emancipation and placing it in historical context. In fact, the study is an extensive review of modern Chinese history in general. *Footbinding, Feminism, and Freedom* is a unique contribution to the growing literature on women's struggle for equality in sport as well as in society. It is a fine book and should be on the reading list of scholars interested in women's sport and emancipation.[39]

This is a book that is grounded firmly in the secondary literature and draws on a wide variety of primary sources. Collins understands the difference between theory and empirically based conclusions. His straightforward prose shows how the sport(s) changed and draws important links between that and the changing nature of Empire, trade unionism, as well as attitudes towards local pride and masculine behaviour. Despite his skill in using rugby's problems and changes to illustrate issues outside of sport, Collins never forgets that none of the administrative or social concerns would mean much if the men who played the game did not care about it and the men, women, boys and girls who watched it were not caught up in both the action on the pitch and the results at the end of the match. Rugby mattered to them and Collins shows us in no uncertain terms why it should matter to us.[40]

This is a splendid book – comprehensive, thoroughly documented, well-written and in many ways quite compelling. It adds a great deal to our understanding of China (already a major force in the world, and surely to become more so as the 21st century unfolds), as well as to ways in which culture, tradition, modernity, politics, and much more shape our conceptions (and the realities) of gender, sport, [and] power. Dong Jinxia is to be congratulated![41]

A central question of all exceptional historical work is how to conceive and describe the ways in which new values and new arrangements for living and bringing meaning into life enter into and inform everyday social and institutional arrangements. This Mangan achieved superbly, combining an eye for the apt and even colourful moment with conceptual understandings drawn from sociology (the sociological process) and anthropology (the use of ritual and symbol). No one has quite done this before, or done it so consistently, although Newsome and Chandos had informally entered the territory. The subject cried out for new approaches. The result was a breakthrough in depicting the development of the public schools and their histories down to our own time.[42]

Writing about the same text, Mangan's *Athleticism in the Victorian and Edwardian Public School*, Allen Guttmann noted: 'When this book appeared in 1981 I read the book and typed six pages of single-spaced notes, concluding with "Marvellous book!"' About the second edition, Guttmann commented: 'I see no reason to alter my first impression of *Athleticism* – "Marvellous book".'[43] Given this, all that seems left for me to add to Guttmann's comment is to say that Mangan has produced not just a marvellous book but a marvellous series. Well done, Tony!

NOTES

1. In contrast Berg Publishers, for example, currently list 21 books on their website, the University of Minnesota Press 13 volumes, SUNY Press 21 and the University of Illinois 31 in its Sport and Society Series.
2. Several books with a publication date prior to this, for example Mangan's own *Athleticism in the Victorian and Edwardian Public School* and Dunning's and Sheard's classic *Barbarians, Gentlemen, and Players* have subsequently been or are being incorporated into the series when second editions or new impressions have been produced.
3. Frank Cass catalogue, *Sport studies: New books and journals* (no date).
4. Jeffrey Richards speaking about Tony Mangan at the celebration of 15 years of Cass books. 27 Nov. 2001. House of Commons, UK.
5. Fan Hong, *Footbinding, Feminism and Freedom: The Liberation of Women's Bodies in Modern China* (London and Portland, OR: Frank Cass, 1997).
6. 'The State, Economics and Sport' in H. Dauncey and G. Hare (eds), *France and the 1998 World Cup: The National Impact of a World Sporting Event* (London and Portland, OR: Frank Cass, 1999).
7. 'Alexandrine Gibb In "No Man's Land of Sport"', in J.A. Mangan and Fan Hong (eds), *Freeing the Female Body: Inspirational Icons* (London and Portland, OR: Frank Cass, 2001).
8. 'Sport and the Masculine Hegemony of the Modern Nation: Welsh Rugby, Culture and Society 1890–1914', in J. Nauright and T.J. Chandler (eds), *Making Men: Rugby and Masculine Identity* (London: Frank Cass, 1996).
9. J. Bale and J. Sang, *Kenyan Running: Movement, Culture, Geography and Global Change* (London and Portland, OR: Frank Cass, 1999).
10. E. Dunning and K. Sheard, *Barbarians, Gentlemen and Players: A Sociological Study of the Development of Rugby Football*, 2nd edn (London and Portland, OR: Frank Cass, forthcoming)
11. R. Cox, D. Russell, and W. Vamplew (eds), *Encyclopedia of British Football* (London and Portland, OR: Frank Cass, 2002).
12. 'Taking Law and Popular Culture Seriously: Theorizing Sport and Law', in S. Greenfield and G. Osborn (eds), *Law and Sport in Contemporary Society* (London and Portland, OR: Frank Cass, 2001).
13. 'Breaking Bounds: Alice Profé, Radical and Emancipationist', in Mangan and Hong, *Freeing the Female Body*.
14. D. Booth, *The Race Game: Sport and Politics in South Africa* (London and Portland, OR: Frank Cass, 1998).
15. 'Body Shapes: The Role of the Medical Establishment in Informing Female Exercise and Physical Education in Nineteenth Century North America', in J. Mangan and R. Park (eds), *From 'Fair Sex' to Feminism: Sport and the Socialization of Women in the Industrial and Post-Industrial Eras* (London: Frank Cass, 1987).
16. 'Foreword', in Cox, Russell, and Vamplew, *Encyclopedia of British Football*.
17. 'Supporters Direct: "Why We're Backing It"', in S. Hamil, J. Michie, C. Oughton, and S. Warby (eds), *The Changing Face of the Football Business: Supporters Direct* (London and Portland, OR: Frank Cass, 2000).
18. 'Foreword', in Hamil, Michie, Oughton, and Warby, *The Changing Face of the Football Business*.
19. Hong, *Footbinding, Feminism and Freedom*; Mangan and Hong, *Freeing the Female Body*; J.A. Mangan and Fan Hong (eds), *Sport in Asian Society: Past and Present* (London and Portland, OR: Frank Cass, 2003).
20. Dong Jinxia, *Women, Sport and Society in Modern China: Holding Up More Than Half the Sky* (London and Portland, OR: Frank Cass, 2002).
21. P. Dimeo and J. Mills (eds), *Soccer in South Asia: Empire, Nation, Diaspora.* (London and Portland, OR: Frank Cass, 2001).
22. Berg differs in this respect in that its focus is more balanced, with a number of North American, British and European authors.
23. H. Dauncey and G. Hare (eds), *The Tour de France, 1903–2003: A Century of Sporting Structures, Meanings and Values* (London and Portland, OR: Frank Cass, 2003).

24. I make this claim based on a search of the SPORT Discus database, which revealed two joint authored articles: 'World Cup France '98: Metaphors, Meanings and Values', *International Review for the Sociology of Sport*, 35 (2000), 331–47, and 'La Commercialisation du Football', *Sociétés et représentation*, 7 (1998), 265–80, plus an online article by Hare '"Get Your Kit On for the Lads": Adidas Versus Nike, The Other World Cup', *Sociology of Sport on Line (SOSOL)*, 2, 2, online at http://physed.otago.ac.nz/sosol/v2i2/v2i2a1.htm.

25. Fan Hong, *Footbinding, Feminism and Freedom*; Dong Jinxia, *Women, Sport And Society in Modern China*.

26. See J. Kolatch, *Sport, Politics and Ideology in China* (New York: Jonathan David Publishers, 1972); J. Riordan (ed.), *Sport Under Communism: The USSR, Czechoslovakia, the GDR, China, Cuba* (Montreal: McGill-Queen's University Press, 1978); J. Riordan and R. Jones, *Sport and Physical Education in China* (London: E & FN Spon, 1999); S. Brownell, *Training the Body for China: Sports in the Moral Order of the People's Republic* (Chicago, IL: University of Chicago Press, 1995).

27. P. Darby *Africa, Football and FIFA: Politics, Colonialism and Resistance* (London and Portland, OR: Frank Cass, 2002); Bale and Sang, *Kenyan Running*; D. Booth, *The Race Game*.

28. J. Gemmell, *The Politics of South African Cricket* (London and Portland, OR: Frank Cass, forthcoming).

29. For example, Liz Crolley and David Hand, *Football, Europe and the Press* (London and Portland, OR: Frank Cass, 2002), and Jack Williams, *Cricket and England: A Cultural and Social History of the Inter-war Years* (London and Portland, OR: Frank Cass, 1999).

30. Stephen G. Wieting (ed.), *Sport and Memory in North America* (London and Portland, OR: Frank Cass, 2001) being the exception.

31. D. Bell, International Games Archives (Oct. 2001), online at www.internationalgames.net/alphalist.htm.

32. Maurice Roche, *Mega-events and Modernity: Olympics and Expos in the Growth of Global Culture* (London: Routledge, 2000).

33. Matthew J. Burbank, Gregory D. Andranovich and Charles H. Heying, *Olympic Dreams: The Impact of Mega-events on Local Politics* (Boulder, CO: Lynne Rienner Publications, 2001).

34. See http://news.bbc.co.uk/2/hi/business/1961343.stm

35. See www.goethe.de/in/download/arabisch/kirchcollapse-e.pdf.

36. See Geneviève Rail (ed.), *Sport and Postmodern Times* (Albany, NY: State University of New York Press, 1998); Debra Shogan, *The Making of High Performance Athletes: Discipline, Diversity and Ethics* (Toronto: University of Toronto Press, 1999); David Andrews, *Michael Jordan, Inc.* (Albany, NY: State University of New York Press, 2001).

37. John K. Walton, review of Mike Huggins, *Flat Racing and British Society, 1790–1914: A Social and Economic History*, *Journal of Social History* (Winter 2001), 489.

38. Wolfgang Weber, review of Meinander and Mangan's *The Nordic World in Culture, Sport, Society*, 3, 130–1.

39. Ying Wu, review of Hong, *Footbinding, Feminism and Freedom*, *Journal of Sport History*, 26, 608–10.

40. Charles Korr, review of Collins, *Rugby's Great Split: Class, Culture and the Origins of Rugby League Football*, *Albion*, 31, 335–6.

41. Roberta Park, personal correspondence to Jonathan Manley, editor, Frank Cass, 24 Aug. 2002.

42. Sheldon Rothblatt, 'Foreword' to J.A. Mangan, *Athleticism in the Victorian and Edwardian Public School*, 2nd edn (London and Portland, OR: Frank Cass, 2000).

43. Allen Guttmann, review of Mangan, *Athleticism in the Victorian and Edwardian Public School*.

J.A. Mangan:
Innovating Down South American Way

LAMARTINE DACOSTA

In his ground-breaking book *The Games Ethic and Imperialism*, J. A. Mangan introduced the theme of the export of 'manliness' in British sport with a careful qualification: 'The story in its full complexity cannot be told here, it is intended that further instalments will appear in due course.' In 2001, in *Europe, Sport, World: Shaping Global Societies*, once again he drew the attention of his readers to the fact that regarding the history of 'global sports society' much remained to be told. However, he also once again demonstrated his originality: 'The stories here have not been told before in this form nor in a single collection.'

This careful dialogue between the intricacy and volume of the past and the need to acknowledge its barely explored nature, has been Mangan's style as an author. And the style is the man; Mangan has also been an outstanding international editor, giving persistent warnings to authors under his aegis of 'incompleteness' to be overcome.

Given this opportunity to represent J.A. Mangan, man, author and editor, what I intend to do, therefore, is to briefly sketch my experience promoting his exchanges with his South American academic friends and colleagues. Behind this intention lies my admiration for his intellectual virtue of mapping out sport as cultural subject-matter – a view wholly in line with my own personal scholastic inclinations.

A sense of 'incompleteness' blended with a cultural interpretation of sport explains Mangan's concern with a world view to be pursued in conjunction with regional or local nuances. Consequently, although he has never given up his deep interest in the British Empire, he has created a network of historical inquiries around the world clearly stimulated by a desire for synthesis, revealed by a remark in his recent book mentioned above, *Europe, Sport, World: Shaping Global Societies*: 'The common sports of modern political, economic and cultural systems, whatever the accidental or deliberate variations, now ensure the existence of societies which are as much global as insular. As yet there is no such thing as a Global Society, but societies are increasingly global.'

Interestingly, a 'locally global society' was Mangan's first experience of South America in 1995, in Iguazu, a triangular area encompassing Argentina, Brazil and Paraguay, which operates as a free-trade zone. In former times, Iguazu was famous for its waterfalls, considered the biggest in the world. It also hosted, in the seventeenth century, an experiment in self-government, with the Jesuits joining Indian nations in independent *missiones*. Today, tax-free commerce promotes self-government but partly in order to facilitate smuggling, gambling and illegal business. Thus Chinese and Arab merchants, in addition to American tycoons, control the shopping and the casino's activities. Could we have found a better setting for discussions on the globalizing trends of sport?

Into a 1940s Hollywood scenario came J.A. Mangan, in company with John Andrews – president of Federation Internationale de Educacion Physique (FIEP). We were there to attend a FIEP congress. Andrews introduced me to Mangan. That first contact gave me the immediate impression that he was keen to include a suitable South American scholar in his international network. The days in the Casablanca-like hotel offered opportunities for confirming a personal realization of Mangan's strong concern with 'incompleteness' in sports studies. Very probably, this has given birth to a personal ambition, illustrated by his intelligent emphasis on both individualistic idiosyncrasies and recurrent patterns in intercultural relationships. Mangan's constant search for pieces of knowledge that could enable him to complete an understanding of sport in global culture, it seems to me, reveals itself, in one form, as a visionary editorial task. During the Iguazu discussions I had early come to the conclusion that Mangan was quite simply an exceptional, all-encompassing editor in the field of sports studies.

It should be added that I was seduced at once by the invitation and the idea, as he put it, of 'opening up your global regional area to the English speaking world'. The academic situation of Brazil in terms of sport and physical education – and the situation in some other parts of South America too – has needed that kind of suggestion in recent years. Brazilian sports academic potential, in particular, is amazingly extensive and insufficiently acknowledged by international scholars and their educational and research institutions. Put succinctly, the country has 240 faculties, 14 masters and four doctoral programmes on physical education and sport. As a result, Brazilian academic production in this area is often considered the biggest among Third World nations, with a possible exception of China. Regrettably, only a few authors have successfully overcome both the post-colonial prejudices of First World peers and, more importantly, the barrier of the English language as required by international journals and books on sport matters.

Mangan, of course, as noted already, also had other terms of reference for his South American commitments. Listening to his fascinating words when analysing the English influence on sport all over the continent, it became clear that he was searching for cultural meanings, not simply the usual limited sporting causes and effects and impacts and links. The case of Argentina, in particular, revealed Mangan's alluring engagement with the theme of the cultural significance of the dissemination of the Anglo-Saxon ideology of athleticism. In the end, seduced willingly in the 'time capsule' atmosphere of the Casablanca-like hotel, I made a deal with Mangan to help him open up South America to the international history of sport.

The consequences of this deal came about in due course. We both decided that the extension of his proposal throughout the South American academic environment should commence by using the history of sport congresses held in Brazil. This option might be regarded as the beginning of Mangan's experiment as a sports history proselytizer in Latin America – in some ways similar to his compatriots' deeds when spreading moral muscularity in Britain's Empire.

There was sound sense in choosing the Brazilian history of sport congresses. To Brazilian sport historians the chance of access to publishing beyond the national borders was attractive. There was ample material. Since 1995 there have been some 50 to 80 papers presented at the national congresses on sport history.[1]

This vigorous creativity did not already occur in other South American countries, and only a few sport historians from neighbouring countries participated in the Brazilian surge. With the seed already sown in Iguazu, Mangan won over his new South American academic colleagues and indeed others. In time other European and North

American historians and sociologists also came to regional congresses. In 1996 and 1997, Eric Dunning, Mike Featherstone and Birger Petersen participated in the Belo Horizonte and Maceio congresses, located respectively in central and northern Brazil. The inspirational cultural patchwork 'carpet', suggested in Iguazu, was being woven.

While most of these distinguished visitors limited their participation to the congresses, Dunning and Mangan remained in the country in order to give seminars in the University of Campinas (São Paulo State) and the University Gama Filho (Rio de Janeiro), the two centres of historical excellence that emerged from the Brazilian surge of sport history in the 1990s. At first glance, these locations represent choices derived from opportunities, but clearly there were at that time two schools of thought in historical inquiry: sociological history (São Paulo) and cultural history (Rio de Janeiro).

Mangan, of course, was especially welcome in Gama Filho where he discussed his academic interests, strategies and ambitions. In turn, Dunning in São Paulo tried to root Norbert Elias's theories more deeply in the 'brave new world' of the southern hemisphere. This Anglo-Brazilian connection became stable, at least as regards Mangan, who energetically applied his successful global cultural approach to opening up the 'regional area to the English speaking world'. Here is a summary of his South American saga:

1995: Initial discussions in Iguazu.

1996: Seminars and discussions in Gama Filho with professors and students from the masters and doctorate programme in physical education. Practical result: an investigation on sport in mid-nineteenth-century Rio de Janeiro conducted by Vitor Melo, the programme's youngest student, whom Mangan supported and encouraged and eventually published in *IJHS*. Journey to Belo Horizonte (central region of Brazil) in order to participate in the Brazilian Congress of Sports History. Practical result: the commencement of Lamartine DaCosta's research on the fascist influence on Brazilian sport. Later this investigation was summarized and edited by Mangan for *Superman Supreme – Global Fascism*, published in 2000.

1998: Gama Filho discussions with a focus on the editorial requirements of submitted texts; participation at the Brazilian Congress of Sports History located in Rio de Janeiro. Practical result: Sebastian Votre – one of Gama Filho professors – became a visiting scholar at Mangan's International Research Centre at Strathclyde

University for post-doctorate research on the theme of women and sport in Brazil. Lamartine DaCosta joined the *IJHS* international editorial board to improve contacts with Latin American sport historians.

1999: Sebastian Votre finished his research in Glasgow. Practical result: an association of Votre with Ludmila Mourao in joint research dedicated to women and sport hosted by the Gama Filho postgraduate programme. The association widened into a research group and it is now one of the most productive in Brazil. Eventually, Votre and Mourao published the early products of their inquiries in *Freeing the Female Body: Inspirational Icons* edited by J.A. Mangan and Fan Hong in 2001. Lamartine DaCosta recommended that Cesar Torres, a sports historian from Argentina, join the *IJHS* international board.

2000: Mangan returned to Gama Filho and then travelled to Rio Grande do Sul (the south of Brazil) to participate again in the Brazilian Congress of Sports History held in Gramado and located in the largest German colonization area in South America. Happily, this time Mangan made contacts with sport historians from Argentina, Chile and Uruguay and in an opening address gave a fascinating presentation on the English influence on Argentina's sport. Practical result: Mangan helped lead the recovery of the German sport memory in southern Brazil, joining my own and Gertrud Pfister's efforts to carry forward the investigations made by Leomar Tesche, another young sport historian from Rio Grande do Sul; and from Gramado's contacts and discussions a plan for a book emerged: *Sport in Latin American Society: Past and Present*.

2001: The research of Leomar Tesche and Artur Blasco Rambo, edited and enriched by Mangan and DaCosta, became the opening chapter of the book *Europe, Sport, World: Shaping Global Societies*. In this volume, *inter alia*, Mangan outlined the complex web of cultural meanings of South American sport from its origins involving British, German and Italian influences.

2002: *Sport in Latin American Society: Past and Present*, edited by J.A. Mangan and L.P. DaCosta was published by Frank Cass, bringing together many of the topics discussed in Iguazu earlier in 1995, but reinforced by new interpretations and authors.

2003: South American material will appear in Mangan's new Frank Cass journal *Soccer and Society*, as well as in his *International Journal of the History of Sport*.

What is next? Will Mangan's sense of 'incompleteness' continue to prevail and will we see the further and fuller incorporation of South America into sports global web of cultural meanings? It is to be hoped so. And if so, it will be due in no small measure to Mangan's impressive efforts.

NOTE

1. See *ISHPES Bulletin*, 15 (1998).

11

East Meets West and West Meets East: Celebrating *The International Journal of the History of Sport*

HA NAM-GIL

Every nation, of course, has its own culture, and modern sport is now invariably an integral part of that culture. The various Asian nations have developed their unique modern physical cultures and social anthropologists, sociologist and sports historians among others have increasingly studied these cultures. Today the world is becoming a 'global village' and now is the time for studies of all physical cultures to become available to inhabitants of that village. Efforts are now required from East and the West to understand each other's physical cultures. And what the East and the West need most is the publication of reliable journals. The publication of *The International Journal of the History of Sport*, or *IJHS*, has opened up new possibilities for the interchange of studies of Eastern and Western physical cultures.

For the past two decades the *IJHS* has been invaluable in disseminating the history of the sport of the world across the world. Moreover, the character of the *IJHS* has brought a new quality to the publication of the work of the world's sports historians. The *IJHS* does not merely look at facts and records, but approaches sport from a political, cultural and social points of view. This has provided a new analytical dimension to sports history.

The growth of the *IJHS* into an exceptional historian journal has been largely due to the determination and effort of one remarkable scholar, Professor J.A. Mangan. Despite many difficulties, Professor Mangan has nurtured the *IJHS* with unflagging spirit and with an uncompromising academic integrity. As I know personally, he is fine educator, historian and editor. I was fortunate to have the experience of spending some time observing his work at his Strathclyde University research centre, the International Research Centre for Sport, Socialisation and Society. There

I witnessed his academic quality, passion and determination. Now, with *IJHS* celebrating its 20th anniversary, I would like to applaud Professor Mangan for his vital role in, and dedication to, the growth of what is generally regarded, certainly in Asia, as the finest journal of its kind.

The *IJHS* has had a significant impact on the Asian sports history academic community. Due to Western imperialism in the late nineteenth century and the associated expansionist policies of various European countries and the United States, Asia, of course, became Westernized in many things; indeed, many Western countries became influenced by Asia. Sports culture was no exception to this two-way influence. During the 1900s, British and American sports began streaming into Asia and as a result Western sport became an integrated part of Asian nations, their education, cultures and societies. Studies of the history of the process by which Western sport came to Asia are still rare. The *IJHS* has come to play a key role both ensuring an understanding of the introduction of Western sport into Asian nations and reciprocally the introduction of the sports of Asia to the West. It has made an invaluable contribution to the process of disseminating studies of both Western and Eastern sports cultures. Professor Mangan has been ever present in commissioning, stimulating and encouraging this dissemination.

The point should also be made that Professor Mangan and the *IJHS* have greatly influenced the evolution of the Korean sports history community. In our case, three main sports sectors have been present during the twentieth century: Korean traditional sports such as taekwondo and ssireum (Korean style wrestling); organized sports from the United Kingdom such as badminton, tennis, football and hockey; and organized sports from the United States of America such as basketball, handball and baseball.

In the early 1900s, traditional Korean sports as well as British and American sports were widespread in the Korean education system and society. However, after the Second World War the influence of American sports became stronger. Korea became more Americanized, as contact with America was more frequent than with Europe. Consequently, the American sports of baseball, basketball and handball became more popular among the Korean public. As a result, an understanding of British sport was shallow and sports historians undertaking studies of European sports were rare. As the *IJHS* became available in Korea, however, the interest in European sports history increased. During the 1980s articles on British history could not be found in the *Korean Journal of Sports History*, but in the 1990s articles on British sports history were published more frequently. In this process Professor Mangan and the *IJHS* had a major influence. Furthermore, various other publications by Professor Mangan – *Athleticism in the Victorian and Edwardian Public School*; *Pleasure, Profit, Proselytism: British Culture and Sport at Home and Abroad, 1700–1914*; *Manliness and Morality*; *The Cultural Bond: Sports, Empire, Society*; *The Games Ethic and Imperialism* – all played a vital role in bringing about an awareness of British sport to Korean sports and cultural historians.

Of the many contributions the *IJHS* and Professor Mangan have made to the Korean sports history community, perhaps the most exceptional is that of introducing Korean sports history to the world through the medium of attractive readable English. Until 1994, articles on Korean sports history had not been published in the English language. In the *IJHS*, 'A Curious Conjunction: Sport, Religion and Nationalism', 'The Knights of Korea', 'Hwarangdo, Militarism and Nationalism', 'Ideology, Politics, Power: Korean Sport–Transformation, 1945–92' have all appeared in the 1990s and have played a key role in presenting the history of Korean sport to the English-speaking world.

Finally, it would be most remiss of me if I did not strongly applaud publicly Professor Mangan's recent important Foreword to *Soccer in South Asia*, in which he stresses the need for Asian commentators in English-language publications on Asian sport in an attempt to balance the confident, but not always sufficiently knowledgeable, Western commentators who set themselves the task, too often without a knowledge of the languages – and therefore the archives as well as important secondary works in the indigenous languages. This is a statement by Professor Mangan that is widely welcomed by myself and my Korean colleagues.

For 20 years the *IJHS* and its founding editor Professor Mangan have contributed to the development and interchange of Western and Eastern sports history. The twenty-first century is the era of a global sports culture. Sport is not only becoming an integral part of our lives, but sports history is also becoming an important study in the academic world. Professor Mangan has played a major part in this. Through the *IJHS*, as well as his own writings, Professor Mangan will leave a distinguished mark on the history of world sport. Once again, I send my congratulations and my respects to Professor Mangan for his notable accomplishments.

12

Sensitive Supervision:
Student Appreciations

FAN HONG

Fan Hong was an editor of the *Journal of Sports Culture and History*, published in Beijing by the Sports Ministry in the 1980s. She was executive secretary to the Chinese Society for History of Physical Education and Sport in Beijing from 1987 to 1990. She obtained her BA and MA at Chinese universities. From 1991 to 1994 Fan Hong was a Ph.D. student of Professor J.A. Mangan at Strathclyde University in Britain.

'When I began my research I was only too well aware that it would not be easy. There was a long and difficult linguistic, conceptual and empirical route to travel. In particular, I had to climb a steep linguistic "track". In this journey through the landscape of the English language my guide, Professor Mangan, supported my faltering steps with the attention to my efforts that every student hopes for. He saved me from stumbles beyond reckoning, and when I slipped he quietly and firmly picked me up. It was his quality of supervision: speedy in response, meticulous in textual scrutiny and always readily available for discussion and continually encouraging and enthusiastic in approach, which ensured that I completed my journey. I would like to express my deep gratitude to Professor Mangan, who is always my mentor. Without his guidance, help and support I would never have come this far.'

Fan Hong is now reader in the Department of Sport Sciences at De Montfort University in England. She has written extensively in academic journals. Her previous books in English are *Footbinding, Feminism and Freedom: The Liberation of Women's Bodies in Modern China* (1997); *Freeing the Female Body: Inspirational Icons* (2001) (co-edited with J.A. Mangan) and *Sport in Asian Society: Past and Present* (2002) (also co-edited with J.A. Mangan).

J.A. Mangan: Guru of International Sports History

ANDREW RITCHIE

When I first approached Professor J.A. Mangan at Strathclyde University, I was doing a one-year M.Phil. at Edinburgh University, researching the life of my great-great-grandfather, Dr John Ritchie, a politically engaged Presbyterian minister in mid-nineteenth-century Scotland, who campaigned against slavery and took a radical stand in the 'voluntary controversy' (Who should appoint ministers? What is the nature of the pastoral relationship between ministers and congregation? Where does spiritual authority ultimately reside?). At the same time, I was not sure that my career was destined to lie in the direction of ecclesiastical history! This was because, for the whole of my life, I have been involved in cycling, and for 25 years of my life I had been exploring and researching the extraordinary nineteenth-century documentation of cycling as a sport, an industry and a social phenomenon that redefined nineteenth-century social and transportation patterns.

On that first meeting, Professor Mangan took me to lunch in the faculty dining room, and in his clear, forthright manner, filled me in on the entire structure of the British sports history world and the state of play at Strathclyde University, and also intuited the fact that my publishing record and my passionate interest in cycling were leading me fairly evidently in the future direction of academic sport history rather than Scottish political/ecclesiastical history. A couple of weeks later, I received a fax from him which said simply, 'You have a Ph.D. berth here if you want it.' A few months later, after I had written my proposal, I received the good news that a Strathclyde University Faculty Studentship was mine for three years to enable me to write my dissertation.

Since then, I have been a part of Professor Mangan's *IJHS* editorial team, and have read and edited articles on a wide range of subjects, from chariot-racing in ancient Constantinople, to the history of water polo, to black soccer players in England and the history of cricket in India. All this has been icing on the cake, so to speak, to my main business, my Ph.D. dissertation (now completed) whose title is 'Bicycle Racing: Sport, Technology and Modernity, 1867–1903', which will soon be published by Frank Cass in Professor Mangan's 'Sport in the Global Society' series.

Cycling occupies a somewhat unusual position among sports. It is an old sport, originating at the moment of birth of the modern bicycle in the late 1860s; it is an extraordinarily well documented sport; it is even a sport about which quite a lot of secondary texts have been written through the years – and yet, for a variety of reasons which there is not space to go into here, it is not a sport that has been well explored from a critical and academic point of view. Professor Mangan understood from the start, even though he did not know the history of cycling per se, what an important niche it occupied in the overall picture of late nineteenth-century sport and how necessary it was that the research be done and the story be told.

On a more personal note, I think other students and ex-students of Professor Mangan's will agree with me that, as a supervisor and as a mentor, he must surely be unrivalled. He is a master of the carrot-and-stick approach – praising when it is earned and criticizing when it is necessary, and always to good purpose. This had led to the extraordinary publishing success of his students and is illustrative of the quality of his supervision. Above all, he is always encouraging, and there is never a moment when you feel that he has lost his interest in you as a student or in your academic future, or that any little detail of what you are doing might have slipped his memory. While I have been rewriting the first draft of my thesis, Professor Mangan's comments have invariably been apposite and always required serious consideration. His capacity for creative, editorial and supervisory work is phenomenal. I have this abiding mental picture of him sitting in his office, surrounded by piles of published works and unpublished works in manila folders, juggling a dozen balls without letting any of them drop to the ground!

CALLUM McKENZIE

Callum McKenzie took a first degree at Manchester Metropolitan University, England and then completed a graduate degree at Manchester University, England. He is currently completing his doctoral degree at Strathclyde University, Scotland. After a period of teaching on the Scottish Borders, he is moving closer to Hebridean family roots with a relocation to Inverness. He studies hunting and was a contributor to the *Encyclopedia of British Sport* (2000).

'"From tautology to tightness." Tony Mangan's battle cry for academic excellence remains germane to my own academic shortcomings! It also explains his continued success in the battlefield of sports history and his permanence in research and publishing. His uncompromisingly assertive attitude has ensured a rigorous and highly acclaimed approach to publication in an increasingly competitive genre. That Tony Mangan remains a key player in sport history reflects his ability to motivate students and publishers alike. The forthcoming publication of my doctoral thesis, when completed with Tony, is clear evidence of his continued attraction as an academic.'

DONG JINXIA

Dong Jinxia is an associate professor and the director of a newly established research centre on women, sport and society at Peking University. She is also an international gymnastics judge. She obtained her doctoral degree from the University of Strathclyde, Scotland in 2001. She has published numerous books and articles in English and Chinese.

'In the mid-1990s, knowing very little of Western culture and with limited English skills, but with the realization that English was the academic global language of the twentieth century, and very likely to remain so in the twenty-first century, I decided to pursue a doctoral degree in the West to advance my career intellectually – like many other Chinese at the time.

'I was aware of Professor Mangan, his International Research Centre and his many publications on sport and society. He was well known in China. I was also aware of his writings on women, sport and emancipation at the academic conference prior to the Seoul Olympics in 1988. He seemed the logical choice as the supervisor for my own intended thesis on women, sport and society in China. I was delighted when I gained a research place at his centre. However, to be absolutely honest, delight was quickly tempered with concern when I discovered just how stony the path ahead was going to be for me. In effect, I was on my own personal academic 'Long March' on a pathway that climbed up and up and was not only stony but slippery! And in truth, I found Professor Mangan a hard if conscientious and committed taskmaster. His standards were high. His stress on originality, rigour and thoroughness seemed at times too much.

'What I completely failed to realize initially was that his demands of me were determined by doctoral standards in British universities, and by his own determination to ensure that since I had sacrificed so much to achieve my personal ambitions, I was not going to go away from his centre empty-handed. If he said to me once then he said it a thousand times: "I will see you through!"

'Mine was a lengthy journey. Sometimes I questioned my own abilities. Other times I questioned his demands. What sustained me was my supervisor's commitment to my success. He backed me – intellectually and spiritually. Wonderfully, in the end his judgment proved sound. When the pieces of the thesis became whole, and Frank Cass publication swiftly followed – only then did I fully recognize what had been fairly achieved, how far I had travelled, how high I had climbed.

'Under Professor Mangan's mentorship, my intellectual competence, my proficiency in English had all improved beyond measure. More than this, I learnt that determination, perseverance and belief are essential qualities for success. Without any doubt, Professor J.A. Mangan had, and still has, a special influence on my academic career. His lessons are lasting.

'I want to say therefore, to Professor Mangan: "You are a most exceptional supervisor. Your intelligence, support and strength sustained me and ensure my success. Your influence is permanent. You are a lifelong supervisor. Thank you."'

J.A. Mangan: Man, Cult, Phenomenon

BORIA MAJUMDAR

I

When asked to comment on Professor J.A. Mangan's contribution to the development of sports history in South Asia, I was pleased. Mangan's scholarship had, almost unknowingly, become a part of my growing up, shaping my understanding of the importance of sport in studying South Asian history and vice versa. Mangan had, almost single handedly (though, of course, unknown to himself), inspired me in the study of sport, still considered an esoteric brand of scholarship in India.

Having graduated from Presidency College, Calcutta, one of the premier academic institutions of colonial and post-colonial India and having topped the University of Calcutta merit list in history, I had thought that my innovatory desire to study the social history of Indian sport (cricket) would be welcomed as the opening up of a new and significant field in Indian history. How mistaken I was! When I mentioned to the head of the department at Presidency College my intention to study the cultural history of Indian cricket as my doctoral dissertation, I was told not to waste a good career. I was instructed – almost ordered – to abandon my foolish idea and come back to him once I had thought of a 'proper' history topic. Sport in South Asia was not part of history; it was mere 'leisure' or 'entertainment' which had and has no historical significance.

Having been dismissed thus, I applied for a Rhodes Scholarship, hoping that the importance attached to sport by the Rhodes Scholarship Trust would lead them to look at the project in a different light. Luckily for me, I was offered the scholarship and the opportunity to pursue a doctoral project at Oxford University. I now had an approved project, which from most historians in India evoked only a smirk. Professor Madhavan Palat of the Jawaharlal Nehru University in fact had told me that the Rhodes Scholarship selection committee should not have allowed me to go ahead with such an outrageous project. It was at this point in my career that I read *The Games Ethic and Imperialism* by Professor Mangan. It was this monograph, arguably Mangan's best (I consider it even better than *Athleticism in the Victorian and Edwardian Public School*), which helped me confirm my conviction that sport was not peripheral to understanding the working of Asian/South Asian societies. Rather, it was essential to understanding the evolution of the modern Indian nation state, and a proper understanding of colonial Indian history remains incomplete without reference to sport.

To illustrate the point: existing histories tell us that the Indian middle class and the aristocracy were at loggerheads at all stages during the nationalist struggle. The history of Indian cricket, however, indicates otherwise. For purposes of resistance on the sports field, to meet and defeat British/European sides in their own game, the middle class and the aristocracy had made common cause in Bengal. From the closing years of the nineteenth century both groups had taken the lead in promoting cricket among the masses of the province. Further, while communalism has been looked upon as one of the worst evils to have plagued Indian public life, early Indian cricket in Bombay, in fact, benefited greatly from its communal/sectarian organization. It was this kind of organization that accounted for the tremendous popularity of the Bombay Pentangular, when other zonal/regional tournaments were often played in empty grounds in colonial India. From its very inception the Bombay Pentangular, the foremost cricket tournament in pre-partition India, was a commercial success story, so much so that the gate receipts from the Pentangular were used to pay off the huge debt incurred during the building of the Brabourne Stadium in Bombay, the country's first permanent sporting venue. Despite this, however, the Pentangular remains unmentioned in existing studies of Indian economic history. A denial of the commercial significance of cricket, one of the largest contributors to the national exchequer, renders all existing studies of India's economic development problematic.

II

Mangan's work, from *The Games Ethic and Imperialism* to his recent chapter in *Soccer in South Asia*, charts the trajectory of the evolution of sport in South Asia from a British import in the middle of the nineteenth century to the turn of the century, when it became a site for the contestation of colonial power. His early concern was to record and analyse the importance attached to sport as a pragmatic and altruistic colonial civilizing tool. This is clear from the following description in *The Games Ethic and Imperialism*:

> The Indian public school was created out of a hotch-potch of Victorian motives – imperial calculation, ethnocentric self-confidence and well meaning benevolence. . . . Even in its more socially restricted form, however, the early Indian public school system provides a fascinating illustration of the cultural diffusion of an educational ethic arising out of imperial conquest. And, in only gently modified form, it has survived the imperialist.

In subsequent stages of his career, Mangan has shown equal concern in trying to understand how the games ethic was appropriated and subverted by the colonized in the course of time. His studies cater not only to enthusiasts interested in the history of sport in South Asia but also to those who might be uninterested in sport itself, but are interested in broader themes of South Asian history such as colonialism, nationalism and communalism. His work on Asia should be viewed as part of the growing concern – advanced emphatically, for example, in the series 'Sport in the Global Society', of which he is the founding and general editor – to locate sport within the broader socio-economic processes that shaped colonial and post-colonial societies, a genre of historical scholarship pioneered initially by scholars like Peter Mandle and then subsequently by Mangan.

In his most recent piece on Indian sport, 'Soccer as Moral Training: Missionary Intentions and Imperial Legacies', unquestionably the best contribution to the volume *Soccer in South Asia*, he offers a purposive account of the introduction of football in Kashmir and NWFP in the 1890s. Mangan sees football as a powerful means to an imperial end, i.e. as a moral tool to strengthen the foundations of the British Empire in India. This focus is a continuation of his earlier work, 'Eton in India', and is key to understanding the inception of colonial sports in the subcontinent. In his own words, 'The game was considered by the colonizers to carry with it a series of moral lessons, regarding hard work and perseverance, about team loyalty and obedience to authority and indeed, involving concepts of correct physical development and "manliness".' He illustrates his argument by narrating the experiences of Leighton Pennell in NWFP and Tyndale Biscoe in Kashmir, who, he argues, used soccer as a seductive weapon to win over local populations. This is one side of the story, also revealed of course in his essay 'Eton in India', that undertakes to bring to light the heterogeneity within the broader imperial administrative project. The other side is the need to record and understand the complexity of interpreting indigenous responses to such projects. This is also a fundamental requirement for Mangan. Too many existing studies have looked upon histories of the origin of British sport in the colonies from a limited perspective, as part of the colonial strategy of a civilizing mission, where sport was simply used as a tool of empire. That Mangan is concerned with what happened to the games ethic in subsequent stages is clear when he declares that 'the legacy of the game in the region hints at a more complex story once the game has been adapted and adopted by Indian groups'. Mangan acknowledges that any assessment of the impact of the intentions and programmes of the colonizers as distinct from their purposes 'is a different matter altogether'. Turning the colonial ideology on its head, resistance and subversion were often dominant in the second phase of the histories of British games in the colonies, especially cricket and soccer. It is in understanding the process of subversion of the games ethic that vernacular literature on sport plays a key role, a point raised by Mangan in his series editor's foreword in *Soccer in South Asia*. Mangan's assertion highlights a need for subtlety that should point the way for future scholars.

Mangan thus stands out as not being an ethnocentric Westerner, as some who write South Asian sports history are, and he recognizes the importance of encouraging scholars from the region to comment on the realities of sport in Asia. This is apparent in his foreword to *Soccer in South Asia*, a book, which, he rightly says, is a mere 'stepping stone' to the future. He also, incidentally, mentions the need for a greater number of Asian collection editors and monograph authors in order that the voices of Asia are heard in all the continent's manifestations – political, cultural, social and emotional. Later 'stepping stones', he rightly states, will be put in place by those closer to the cultures, vernaculars and sources, independently and in conjunction with others. This action, Mangan suggests, will advance to advantage the line of stones across the uncrossed stream and develop more adequately the history of sport in South Asia. As early as 1992 Mangan wrote these perceptive words in his prologue to *The Cultural Bond: Sport, Empire, Society* (London: Frank Cass, 1992):

> It is wise to appreciate that there was no culturally monolithic response to attempts to utilize sport as an imperial bond. A major problem that the analyst of ideological proselytism and its cultural consequences should confront is the nature of interpretation, assimilation and adaptation and the extent of resistance and rejection by the proselytised – in a phrase, the extent and form of ideological implementation.

He added: 'Any analyst worth his salt should be aware of cultural discontinuities as well as continuities. The unanticipated consequences of stated intentions are neither unusual nor unreal.' He then stated further: 'The inclusion within our consideration of the nature of sport as an imperial bond of cultural encounters between dominant and subordinate groups certainly provides the opportunity "to place the grand and theatrical discourses of colonial knowledge and control in the context of their often partial and ironic realizations".' Finally, he remarked:

> It has been claimed that cultural analysis breaks up into a disconnected yet coherent sequence of broader sorties with studies

building on other studies, not in the sense that they take up where others leave off but in the sense that, stimulated by earlier stumbling, better informed and better conceptualized, they penetrate deeper into the same things.

III

In conclusion, when I had first reached Oxford, my first major concern, as is with all graduate students, was what my supervisor, Dr David Washbrook, would say about my project. I still remember the day I had first met David in his office at St Antony's College. It was a cold January morning and David presented me in his office with a reading list. He said that if I wanted to understand trends in global sports history writing, I would do well to go through the reading list as fast as I could. This, he said, would allow me place the history of Indian sport/cricket in proper context. To my utter amazement, 70 per cent of the reading list was taken up by J.A. Mangan. It was, therefore, a list the contents of which I had already voraciously devoured – my earliest tribute to a seminal scholar. This contribution to this celebration number constitutes another tribute, happily made.

Select Bibliography of J.A. Mangan

*1. *Physical Education and Sport: Sociological and Cultural Perspectives; an Introductory Reader* (Oxford: Blackwells, 1973).

2. (a) *Athleticism in the Victorian and Edwardian Public School: the Emergence and Consolidation of an Educational Ideology* (Cambridge: Cambridge University Press, 1981).

   (b) Also (Falmer: Falmer Press, 1986).

   (c) Also (London: Frank Cass, 2000) with New Introduction.

3. (a) *The Games Ethic and Imperialism: Aspects of the Diffusion of an Ideal* (London: Penguin/Viking, 1986).

   (b) Also (London: Frank Cass, 1998).

*4. *Manliness and Morality: Middle-Class Masculinity in Britain and America, 1800-1940* edited with James Walvin (Manchester: Manchester University Press, 1987).

*5. *Sport in Africa: Essays in Social History* edited with William J. Baker (New York: Holmes and Meier, 1987).

*6. *From 'Fair Sex' to Feminism: Sport and the Socialization of Women in the Industrial and Post-industrial Eras* edited with Roberta J. Park (London: Frank Cass, 1987).

*7. *'Benefits Bestowed'?: Education and British Imperialism* (Manchester: Manchester University Press, 1988).

*8. *Pleasure, Profit, Proselytism: British Culture and Sport at Home and Abroad, 1700–1914* (London: Frank Cass, 1988).

*9. *Making Imperial Mentalities: Socialisation and British Imperialism* (Manchester: Manchester University Press, 1990).

*10. *The Business of Professional Sports* edited with Paul D. Staudohar with a foreword by Leonard Koppett (Chicago: University of Illinois Press, 1991).

*11. *The Cultural Bond: Sport, Empire, Society* (London: Frank Cass, 1992).

*12. *The Imperial Curriculum: Racial Images and Education in the British Colonial Experience* (London: Routledge, 1993).

*13. *A Significant Social Revolution: Cross-cultural Aspects of the Evolution of Compulsory Education* (London: Woburn Press, 1994).

* = Collection

*14. *Tribal Identities: Nationalism, Europe, Sport* (London: Frank Cass, 1996).

*15. *European Heroes: Myth, Identity, Sport* edited with Richard Holt and Pierre Lanfranchi (London: Frank Cass, 1996).

*16. *The Nordic World: Sport in Society* edited with Henrik Meinander (London: Frank Cass, 1998).

*17. *Shaping the Superman: Fascist Body as Political Icon – Aryan Fascism* (London: Frank Cass, 1999).

*18. *Sport in Europe: Politics, Class, Gender* (London: Frank Cass, 1999).

*19. *Sport in Australasian Society: Past and Present* edited with John Nauright (London: Frank Cass, 2000).

*20. *Superman Supreme: Fascist Body as Political Icon – Global Fascism* (London: Frank Cass, 2000).

*21. *Making European Masculinities: Sport, Europe, Gender* (London: Frank Cass, 2000).

*22. *Freeing the Female Body: Inspirational Icons* edited with Fan Hong (London: Frank Cass, 2001).

*23. *Europe, Sport, World: Shaping Global Societies* (London: Frank Cass, 2001).

*24. *Sport in Latin American Society: Past and Present* edited with Lamartine P. DaCosta (London: Frank Cass, 2002).

*25. *Reformers, Sport, Modernizers: Middle-Class Revolutionaries* (London: Frank Cass, 2002).

*26. *Sport in Asian Society: Past and Present* edited with Fan Hong (London: Frank Cass, 2003).

*27. *Militarism, Sport, Europe: War Without Weapons* (London: Frank Cass, 2003).

*28. *The Cricket World Cup 2003: Cultures in Conflict* edited with Boria Majumdar (London: Frank Cass, 2003).

*29. *Soccer, Women, Sexual Liberation: Kicking Off a New Era* edited with Fan Hong (London: Frank Cass, 2003).

*30. *Ethnicity, Sport, Identity: Struggles for Status* edited with Andrew Ritchie (London: Frank Cass, 2003).

*31. *Disreputable Pleasures: Less Virtuous Victorians at Play* edited with Mike Huggins (London: Frank Cass, 2004).

FORTHCOMING

* *Sport in South Asian Society: Past and Present* edited with Boria Majumdar.
* *A Sport Loving Society: Victorian and Edwardian Middle-Class England at Play.*
* *Sport and Africa: Nationalism, Globalization, Commercialism.*
  Blooding the Male: Imperialism, Masculinity, Hunting edited with Callum McKenzie.
  Soccer Schoolmasters: Pioneering the People's Game Across the Globe with Colm Hickey.

CHAPTERS IN BOOKS

'Some Sociological Concomitants of Secondary School Physical Education: Exploratory Suggestions' in J. A. Mangan (ed.) *Physical Education and Sport: Sociological and Cultural Perspectives* (Oxford: Blackwell, 1973), pp.23–34.

'Athleticism: A Case Study of the Evolution of an Educational Ideology' in Brian Simon and Ian Bradley (eds.) *The Victorian Public School* (Dublin: Gill and Macmillan, 1975), pp.147–67.

'Almond of Loretto: Rebel, Reformer and Visionary' in D. McNair and Nicholas A. Parry (eds), *Reading in the History of Physical Education* (Zwalina: Ahrensburg, 1981), pp.26–34.

'The Grit of our Forefathers': Invented Traditions, Propaganda and Imperialism' in John M. MacKenzie (ed.), *Imperialism and Popular Culture* (Manchester: Manchester University Press, 1986), pp.113–39.

'Social Darwinism and Upper-class Education in Late Victorian and Edwardian England' in J. A. Mangan and James Walvin (eds), *Manliness and Morality: Middle-Class Masculinity in Britain and America, 1800–1940* (Manchester: Manchester University Press, 1987), pp.135–59.

'Ethics and Ethnocentricity: Imperial Education in British Tropical Africa' in William J. Baker and James A. Mangan (eds), *Sport in Africa: Essays in Social History* (New York: Holmes and Meier, 1987), pp.172–95.

'Moralists, Metaphysicians and Mythologists: The "Signifiers" of a Victorian and Edwardian Sub-Culture' in Susan J. Bandy (ed.), *Coreobus Triumphs: The Alliance of Sports and the Arts* (San Diego: San Diego University Press, 1988), pp.142–62.

'Introduction: Imperialism, History and Education' in J. A. Mangan (ed.), *Benefits Bestowed?: Education and British Imperialism* (Manchester: Manchester University Press, 1988), pp.1–22.

'Catalyst of Change: John Guthrie Kerr and the Adaptation of an Indigenous Scottish Tradition' in J. A. Mangan (ed.), *Pleasure, Profit, Proselytism: British Culture and Sport at Home and Abroad, 1700–1914* (London: Frank Cass, 1988), pp.86–104.

'Noble Specimens of Manhood: Schoolboy Literature and the Creation of a Colonial Chivalric Code' in Jeffrey Richards (ed.), *Imperialism and Juvenile Literature* (Manchester: Manchester University Press, 1989), pp.173–94.

'Introduction: Making Imperial Mentalities' in *Making Imperial Mentalities: Socialisation and British Imperialism* (Manchester: Manchester University Press, 1990), pp.1–22.

'The Social History of Sport: Reflections on Some Recent British Developments in Research and Teaching' in David L. Vanderwerken (ed.), *Sport in the Classroom* (London: Associated University Presses, 1990), pp.61–74.

'Prologue: Britain's Chief Spiritual Export: Imperial Sport as Moral Metaphor, Political Symbol and Cultural Bond' in J. A. Mangan (ed.), *The Cultural Bond: Sport, Empire, Society* (London: Frank Cass, 1992), pp.1–10.

'Images for Confident Control: Stereotypes in Imperial Discourse' in J. A. Mangan (ed.), *The Imperial Curriculum: Racial Images and Education in the British Colonial Experience* (London: Frank Cass, 1993), pp.6–22.

'Duty unto Death: English Masculinity and Militarism in the Age of the New Imperialism' in J. A. Mangan (ed.), *Tribal Identities: Nationalism, Europe, Sport* (London: Frank Cass, 1996), pp.10–38.

'Games Field and Battlefield: A Romantic Alliance in Verse and the Creation of Militaristic Masculinity' in John Nauright and Timothy J. L. Chandler (eds.), *Making Men: Rugby and Masculine Identity* (London: Frank Cass, 1996), pp.140–57.

'Muscular, Militaristic and Manly: The British Middle-Class Hero as Moral Messenger' in Richard Holt, J. A. Mangan and Pierre Lanfranchi (eds), *European Heroes: Myth, Identity, Sport* (London: Frank Cass, 1996), pp.28–47.

'Sport in Society: the Nordic World and Other Worlds' in Henrik Meinander and J. A. Mangan (eds), *The Nordic World: Sport in*

Society (London: Frank Cass, 1998), pp.173–97.

'English Elementary Education Revisited and Revised: Drill and Athleticism in Tandem' (with Colm Hickey) in J. A. Mangan (ed.), *Sport in Europe: Politics, Class, Gender* (London: Frank Cass, 1999), pp.63–91.

'The Potent Image and the Permanent Prometheus' (pp.11–22); 'Blind, Strong and Pure: "Proto-Fascism", Male Bodies and Political Tradition' (pp.107–27); 'Icon of Monumental Brutality: Art and the Aryan Man' (pp.128–52) in J. A. Mangan (ed.), *Shaping the Superman: Fascist Body as Political Icon – Aryan Fascism* (London: Frank Cass, 1999).

'The Other Side of the Coin: Victorian Masculinity, Field Sports and English Elite Education' (with Callum McKenzie) (pp.62–85); 'Athleticism in the Service of the Proletariat: Preparation for the English Elementary School and the Extension of Middle Class Manliness' (with Colm Hickey) (pp.112–39) in J. A. Mangan (ed.), *Making European Masculinities: Sport, Europe, Gender* (London: Frank Cass, 2000).

'Prologue: Global Fascism and the Male Body: Ambitions, Similarities and Dissimilarities' (pp.1–27); 'Militarism, Sacrifice and Emperor Worship: The Expendable Male Body in Fascist Martial Culture' (with Takeshi Komagome) (pp.181–204); 'Epilogue: Prometheus: Past, Present and Future' (pp.227–36) in J. A. Mangan (ed.), *Superman Supreme: Fascist Body as Political Icon – Global Fascism* (London: Frank Cass, 2000).

'A Pioneer of the Proletariat: Herbert Milnes and the Games Cult in New Zealand' (with Colm Hickey) in J. A. Mangan and John Nauright (eds), *Sport in Australasian Society: Past and Present* (London: Frank Cass, 2000), pp.31–44.

'Missionaries to the Middle Classes' in Heather Holmes (ed.), *Scottish Life and Society: Education: A Compendium of Scottish Ethnology*, Volume 11 (East Linton: Tuckwell Press in association with The European Ethnological Research Centre, 2000), pp.415–34.

'A Martyr for Modernity: Qui-Jin Feminist, Warrior and Revolutionary' (with Fan Hong) (pp.27–54); 'Epilogue – Prospects for the New Millennium: Women, Emancipation and the Body' in J. A. Mangan and Fan Hong (eds), *Freeing the Female Body: Inspirational Icons* (London: Frank Cass, 2001), pp.237–50.

'Confucianism, Imperialism, Nationalism: Modern Sport, Ideology and

Korean Culture' (with Ha Nam-Gil) (pp.49–76); 'Globalization, the Games Ethic and Imperialism: Further Aspects of the Diffusion of an Ideal' (with Colm Hickey) (pp.105–30) in J. A. Mangan (ed.), *Europe, Sport, World: Shaping Global Societies* (London: Frank Cass, 2001).

'Soccer as Moral Training: Missionary Intentions and Imperial Legacies' in Paul Dimeo and James Mills (eds), *Soccer in South Asia: Empire, Nation, Diaspora* (London: Frank Cass, 2001), pp.41–56.

'The Early Evolution of Modern Sport in Latin America: A Mainly English Middle Class Inspiration?' in J. A. Mangan and Lamartine P. DaCosta (eds), *Sport in Latin American Society: Past and Present* (London: Frank Cass, 2002), pp.9–42.

'Prologue: Middle-Class "Revolutionaries" in Pursuit of Moral, Physical, Political and Social Health' (pp.1–8); 'Missing Middle-Class Dimensions: Elementary Schools, Imperialism and Athleticism' (with Colm Hickey) (pp.73–90); '"Golden Boys" of Playing Field and Battlefield: Celebrating Heroes – "Lost" Middle-class Women Versifiers of the Great War' (pp. 134–61); 'Radical Conservatives: Middle-class Masculinity, the Shikar Club and Big Game Hunting' (with Callum McKenzie) (pp.185–209); 'Epilogue: The History of Modern European Sport as a History of Modern European Ideas' in J. A. Mangan (ed.), *Reformers, Sport, Modernizers: Middle-Class Revolutionaries* (London: Frank Cass, 2002).

'Prologue: Combative Sports and Combative Societies' (pp.1–9); 'Lasting Legacy? Spartan Life as a Germanic Educational Ideal: Karl Otfried Müller and *Die Dorier*' (with Orestis Kustrin) (pp.28–45); 'Military Drill – Rather more than "Brief and Basic": English Elementary Schools in English Militarism' (with Hamad S. Ndee) (pp.65–96); '"Pig Sticking is the Greatest Fun": Martial Conditioning on the Hunting Fields of Empire' (with Callum McKenzie) (pp.97–119); 'Epilogue: Many Mansions and Many Architectural Styles' (pp.281–6) in J. A. Mangan (ed.), *Militarism, Sport, Europe: War Without Weapons* (London: Frank Cass, 2003).

'Imperial Origins: Christian Manliness, Moral Imperatives and Pre-Sri Lankan Playing Fields – Beginnings' (pp.11–34); 'Imperial Origins: Christian Manliness, Moral Imperatives and Pre Sri Lankan Playing Fields – Consolidation' (pp.35–66); '"Sportsmanship" – English

Inspiration and Japanese Response: F. W. Strange and Chiyosaburo Takeda' (with Ikuo Abe) (pp.99–128); 'Ideology, Politics, Power: Korean Sport – Transformation, 1945–92' (with Ha Nam-Gil) (pp.213–42) in J. A. Mangan and Fan Hong (eds), *Sport in Asian Society: Past and Present* (London: Frank Cass, 2003).

ARTICLES

'"Play Up and Play the Game": Victorian and Edwardian Public School Vocabularies of Motive', *British Journal of Educational Studies*, XXIII, 3 (October 1975), 324–35.

'Almond of Loretto: Scottish Educational Visionary and Reformer' *Scottish Educational Review*, 11, 2 (November 1979), 97–106.

'Philathlete Extraordinary: A Portrait of the Victorian Moralist, Edward Bowen' in *Journal of Sports History*, 9, 3 (Winter 1982), 27–41.

'Imitating their Betters and Disassociating from their Inferiors: Grammar Schools and the Games Ethic in the late Nineteenth and Twentieth Centuries', *Proceedings of the Annual Conference of the History of Education Society of Great Britain* (December 1982), 1–45.

'Hely Hutchinson Almond: Iconoclast, Anglophile and Imperialist', *Scottish Journal of Physical Education*, 12, 3 (August 1984), 38–41.

'"Oars and the Man": Pleasure and Purpose in Victorian and Edwardian Cambridge', *History of Higher Education Annual*, 4 (December 1984), 52–77.

'The Social Construction of Victorian Femininity: Emancipation, Education and Exercise', *The International Journal of the History of Sport*, 6, 1 (May 1989), 1–9.

'Lamentable Barbarians and Pitiful Sheep: Rhetoric of Protest and Pleasure in Late Victorian and Edwardian "Oxbridge"', *Victorian Studies*, 34, 4 (Summer 1991), 473–90.

'Men, Masculinity and Sexuality: Some Recent Literature', Review Essay, *Journal of the History of Sexuality*, 3, 2 (October 1992), 303–14.

'Le Mitico Gentleman: Cotton, de Coubertin e le origini del fair play', *Lancillotto e Nausia: critica e storia dello sport*, XY, 1 (1998), 28–37.

'The End of History Perhaps – But the End of the Beginning for the History of Sport! An Anglo-Saxon Autobiographical Perspective', *Sporting Traditions*, 16, 1 (November 1999), 61–72.

'Aggression and Androgyny: Gender Fusion in and Beyond Sport in the

Post Millennium Era', *Revue Française de Civilisation Britannique*, X, 4 (2000), 137–40.

'Impero, Cristainesimo ed Etica Sporttiva', *Storia Urban*, XXV, 97 (Ottobre-Dicombre 2001), 63–90.

'Football in the New China: Political Statement, Entrepreneurial Enticement and Patriotic Passion' (with Dong Jinxia), *Soccer and Society*, 2, 3 (Autumn 2001), 79–100.

'Ascending then Descending? Women's Soccer in Modern China' (with Dong Jinxia), *Soccer and Society*, 3, 2 (Summer 2002), 1–18.

GUEST EDITOR

'Education and Imperialism: Four Case Studies', *Aspects of Education*, 40 (Hull: University of Hull, 1989).

'Introduction: Coloniser and Colonised: Imperial Formal Education in the Formative Years' (pp.1–10).

ACKNOWLEDGMENT

Thanks are expressed to Gwang Ok for his most helpful assistance in the compilation of this record of publications.

Notes on Contributors

Frank Cass is Chairman of Frank Cass & Co. Ltd, the company he founded in 1957.

Scott A.G.M. Crawford is a professor and graduate co-ordinator in the Department of Physical Education, Eastern Illinois University.

Martin Crotty is a lecturer in history at the University of Queensland. He has published *Making the Australian Male: Middle-Class Masculinity 1870–1920* (2001) and a number of articles concerned with the construction of masculinity, often concerning the role played by sport. His current research focuses on war and Australian society.

Lamartine P. DaCosta is Senior Professor in the Masters and Doctorate Programme of Physical Education at Gama Filho University, Rio de Janeiro. He has written many articles and books, mostly in Portuguese and on sports issues.

Dong Jinxia is a former gymnast and a professor at Peking University. She has been involved in many international and national sports events as organizer, judge or researcher. Her book *Women, Sport and Society in Modern China* was published by Frank Cass in 2003.

Fan Hong is reader in Department of Sports Sciences at De Montfort University in England. She was an editor of the *Journal of Sports Culture and History*, published by the Sports Ministry in Beijing in the 1980s. Her main research interests are in the areas of body, gender and sport with particular reference to China and Asia. Her most recent books in English are *Footbinding, Feminism and Freedom: The Liberation of Women's Bodies in Modern China* (1997) and *Freeing the Female Body: Inspirational Icons*, co-edited with J.A. Mangan (2001).

Ha Nam-Gil is a professor in the College of Education, Department of Physical Education, Gyeongsang National University, Korea.

Vassil Girginov is Senior Lecturer in Leisure and Sport Studies at Luton Business School, University of Luton. He holds masters degrees in sport management from the National Sports Academy, Sofia, and in European Leisure Studies from the universities of Loughborough, Tilburg, Brussels and Bilbao, as well as a Ph.D. from the University of Loughborough. His research interests and publications (including three books) are in the field of the Olympic movement, sport management and policy analysis, and Eastern European sport.

Gigliola Gori has a doctorate in social science and teaches the History of Physical Education and Sport at the Faculty of Motor Sciences at the University of Urbino, Italy. She is a member of the International Society for the History of Physical Education and Sport (ISHPES) and serves on the editorial boards of the *European Sports History Review* and *Acta Kinesiologiae Universitatis Tartuensis*. She is also a founding member of the European Committee for Sport History. Her book *Female Bodies, Sport, Italian Fascism* will be published by Frank Cass in 2004.

Colm Hickey is Deputy Headteacher at St Bernard's Catholic School, High Wycombe. He took his first degree at the former Borough Road College and completed his MA in the History of Education at the University of London, Institute of Education. He has published a number of articles in the fields of athleticism, imperialism and elementary education. He is currently completing his Ph.D. thesis on Athleticism and the London Teacher Training Colleges at the University of Strathclyde.

Mike Huggins is a retired head of post-graduate teacher training at Lancaster University and currently lectures in history at St. Martin's College, Ambleside, Cumbria. He has written widely on the history of sport and leisure in the modern period, most recently *Flat Racing and British Society 1790–1914* (2000). He is currently co-editing, with J.A. Mangan, a volume entitled *Disreputable Pleasures: Less Virtuous Victorians*.

Callum Campbell McKenzie is completing his doctorate under the supervision of J.A. Mangan. He has published articles on the themes of field sports, masculinity, morality and the search for 'order' in the age of imperialism in various international and national academic journals.

Boria Majumdar is completing his doctorate at St John's College, University of Oxford. His collection (edited with J.A. Mangan) *The Cricket World Cup 2003: Cultures in Conflict* is forthcoming.

Jonathan Manley is a graduate of Pembroke College, University of Cambridge. He has worked as an editor for Frank Cass Publishers for 12 years.

Roberta J. Park is Professor Emeritus in the Department of Integrative Biology, University of California. A member of the faculty since 1959, she served as president of the American Academy of Kinesiology and Physical Education, as a vice-president of the International Society for the History of Physical Education and Sport, and on the editorial boards of numerous journals.

Andrew Ritchie had researched and written about the bicycle and sport of cycling for 25 years. He is currently on the editorial board of the *International Journal of the History of Sport* and is completing a book on the origins and growth of bicycle racing between 1865 and 1903. He is the author of *King of the Road* (1975) and *Major Taylor, The Extraordinary Career of a Champion Bicycle Racer* (1996). He is currently completing a book on the history of bicycle racing which will be published by Frank Cass.

Trevor Slack is professor and Canada Research Chair in Sport Management at the University of Alberta in Canada. He was formerly the editor of the *Journal of Sport Management* and is currently the editor of the *European Sport Management Quarterly*. His work has appeared in such journals as *Organization Studies*, *Journal of Sport Management*, *Journal of Management Studies* and *Human Relations*. His current work is on the changes that are occurring in sports organizations in emerging economies and he edited the collection *The Commercialisation of Sport* (forthcoming).

Index